CW00404208

Birmingham Repertory Theatre Company
presets

All That Trouble
That We Had
By Paul Lucas

First Performance at The Door,
Birmingham Repertory Theatre
on Thu 13 May 1999

SUPPORTED BY
THE NATIONAL LOTTERY
THROUGH
THE ARTS COUNCIL
OF ENGLAND

Birmingham City Council WEST
MIDLANDS
ARTS

Providing Theatre for Birmingham

Paddy Irishman, Paddy Englishman and Paddy...?

By Declan Croghan

Thu 4 Feb - Sat 20 Feb

'What we have to do now is to focus our minds on how we are going to get ourselves out of this situation'.

Kevin and Anto are mates. They're getting by; earning a few spondoolicks, cooking enormous fry ups, avoiding the bad pint and trying desperately to understand women.

But last night a good turn turned bad, and now they've stumbled into something much bigger than both of them. The situation is exploding out of all control and their Irish past is about to come crashing in on their London lives.

Declan Croghan's hilarious black comedy looks at freedc and prejudice, heroism and cowardice and asks to whom we owe our true allegiances.

Director: Anthony Clark
Designer: Patrick Connellan
Lighting: Tim Mitchell

**After Dark: Wed 17 Feb
(after the perf)**

Trips

By Sarah Woods

Thu 25 Feb - Sat 20 Mar

'Have you ever wondered why you find a four and a half foot tall yellow cat more comforting than your own friends?'

What happens when you lose your focus in this dazzling new land of opportunity? Nik, John, Hayley, Dan and Glen are off on a night out; drugs, clubs and the fantastic twenty four hour garage. But tonight things are not quite going to plan.

Searching for love, excitement and one infallible business idea they are all about to encounter more than they ever thought possible. And what has Princess Anne got to

do with it all?.
Sarah Woods' bold, funny an technologically astonishing new play combines live performance with video to explore where we are now, ar where we are all heading.

Director: Jeremy Raison
Designer: Kit Surrey

**After Dark: 17 Mar
(after the perf)**

Nightbus

By Peter Cann

Wed 24 Mar - Sat 3 Apr

'I'm not the kind of person things happen to.'

Meet Donna. She's a tour guide on one of those open-topped Birmingham Tour buses and she knows her city. The city of 1001 trades, of the Rotunda and Spaghetti Junction: the city with more parks than Paris, more miles of canal than Venice and less fun than Dudley, or so it seems.

But Donna doesn't care. Hers is a safe life, governed by electronic organisers, regular hours and familiar routes and routines.

But tonight, fate takes a hand in launching Donna on a bus-ride into weird and unfamiliar territory: one of backstreet cosmetic surgeons and genetic engineers, of phoney traffic wardens, hotel receptionists, escaped chimpanzees, terrifying swimming instructors and crazy bargemen - all out to steal Donna's heart.

Using original, live music, five inventive performers will be

brought together in this actio packed comic journey for all the family - beyond the outer margins of the city we know or think we know.

NIGHTBUS is the first of th year's Rep Community Tours funded by the Sir Barry Jackson Trust

Director: Phil Tinline
Designer: Jens Cole

**After Dark: Wed 31 Mar
(after the performance)**

Feb 99 - June 99

'The largest and potentially most important space outside London dedicated exclusively to new work'
The Guardian Guide

Tickets: £9.00
Concs: £7.00
Standby: £5.00
(limited availability)
Mad to Miss Mondays:
£2.99, Under 26's

Produced in association with Soho Theatre Company

Perpetua
By Fraser Grace

Thu 15 Apr - Sat 8 May

'When a person feels betrayed by the law they trust in, they start to feel there is no way to do good 'cept by forcing themselves to do bad'

Are some lives worth more than others? The town of Pensacola, Florida is about to be set alight by the fiercest of battles. A struggle that pits the law of God against the law of the land, and the right to life against the right to choose.

On one side of the city stands May Lake abortion clinic, on the other the headquarters of the pro-life extremists Operation Freedom.

The battle rages and the stakes get higher with potentially murderous consequences.
Fraser Grace's gripping new play challenges our deepest moral beliefs.

Director: Jonathan Lloyd
Designer: Timothy Meaker

After Dark: Wed 28 April
(after the perf)

All That Trouble That We Had
By Paul Lucas

Thu 13 May - Sat 5 Jun

'We're only good people gone slightly desperate'

When you're in despair no action seems too extreme. On one side of a bridge a daughter employs reckless measures to secure the return of her dead mother. On the other side a man reads *Heroes of Crime* and contemplates the craziest of schemes. And always in the background the distant sound of bodies splashing down from the bridge into the river.

But what part does the cheery, cigar smoking postmistress play? And who is the overweight salesman suddenly dropped into their

lives? And are these bizarre happenings really chance, malice or destiny?
All That Trouble That We Had is a darkly comic and vivacious tale of wickedness on the margins of society celebrates the hopeless, the lonely and the unsuccessful, and explores our capricious ability to survive in vicious times.

Director: Anthony Clark
Designer: Nettie Edwards

After Dark: 6 Jun
(After the perf)

In the Main House

10 Days In June
4 Jun - 13 Jun

A celebration of the best theatre, opera and storytelling for 4-14 year olds.

A festival of the very best in live theatre for young people - taking place all over the theatre. Highlights of the festival include a brand new musical with live animation by David Greig - *Danny 306 & Me (4 Ever)*, a fantastic updated version of *The Magic Flute*, a visit from Sooty and his friends plus much more.

Puppets, music, participation, a full programme of workshops and after show events make for a great day out at theatre. For a full schedule of events or to receive your copy of the *10 Days In June* Festival Brochure call Box Office on 0121 236 4455.

Tickets from just £3.50

All That Trouble That We Had

By Paul Lucas

CAST

David Hargreaves Vaughan

Rachel Smith Hannah

Paul Barnhill Leyton

Will Barton Reg

Lucy Briers Margot

Paul Bradley Oliver

Director Anthony Clark

Designer Nettie Edwards

Lighting Designer Tim Mitchell

Stage Manager Niki Ewen

Deputy Stage Manager Ruth Morgan

Assistant Stage Manager Daniel Precious

Production credits
J Sainsburys plc
Thorntons, The Pallasades
Aqua Cool
Dixons
Midlands Packaging
Coca-Cola Schweppes
Energiser UK Ltd
The Diskery
Royal Mail, Birmingham
Starkeys Bakers

Paul Lucas
Author

Paul's first play *Swamp City* was
performed at The Birmingham Rep
Studio in May 1996. His second play
Beautiful Shortsighted Eyes was
workshopped at the Royal National
Theatre Studio in 1997. He has also
written *The Iguanodon* a three-part
series for Radio 4, broadcast in 1997.
He was born in Coventry and currently
lives in Cardiff.

David Hargreaves
Vaughan

Trained: Leeds Teacher Training College, Central School of Speech and Drama

For Birmingham Repertory Theatre: Harvey in *Season's Greetings*; Professor Richie Baker in *The Four Alice Bakers*

Theatre: RSC, National Theatre, Royal Court, Dundee, Hornchurch, Sunderland Billingham, Leeds, Sheffield, Northampton, Bush Theatre, Old Red Lion, Soho Poly, Foco Novo, Riverside Studios, Lyric Hammersmith, Young Vic, Moving Theatre. Most recently Herman in *Kafka's Dick* (Nottingham Playhouse); Seryosha in *Lavochkin 5* (Tron Theatre); Donald in premiere of A *Passionate Woman* (West Yorkshire Playhouse);

West End: Sir Frederick in *The Changing Room* (Royal Court / Duke of Yorks); Antonio in Peter Hall's *Twelfth Night* (Playhouse Theatre); Ron in *Not Now Darling* (Strand Theatre)

TV: Between *Z Cars* in 1962 and *The Passion* to be shown May 1999 he has appeared in over 400 programmes including Alan Clarke's *A Life is Forever*, Michael Apted's *Stronger Than the Sun*. A regular in the series, *Juliet Bravo* and *Making Out*, most recently episodes of *The Bill*, *Peak Practice*, *Heartbeat*, *Casualty*

Radio: Roger in *Mrs Dales' Diary*. Recently Gregory Dawson in *Priestley's Bright Day*; Raskalnikov in Roger Stennett's *The High Frontier*.

Film: *Othello* (Olivier); *Agatha* (Michael Apted); *She's Been Away* (Peter Hall) As Director: *Chekhov's Women* (Lyric Theatre, Hammersmith).

Last year David produced a walks series for HTV.

Rachel Smith
Hannah

Born: Basingstoke

Trained: Manchester Polytechnic School of Theatre

For Birmingham Repertory Theatre: *Rough*

Theatre: The Governor's Wife in *The Caucasian Chalk Circle* (The Library Theatre Manchester); *I of a Needle* (King's Head London); *Scouse* (The Everyman, Liverpool); *Beautiful Shortsighted Eyes* (National Theatre Studio); Kitty in *Anna Karenina* (Chester Gateway); Gwendolen in *The Importance of Being Earnest* (Manchester Royal Exchange); Cordelia in *King Lear* (Kaboodle Theatre Company, National Tour)

TV: *Where the Heart Is* (United Broadcasting); *The Celluloid World of Dezmond Rezillo* (BBC Wales); *The Lord of Misrule* (Hat Trick Productions); *How We Used To Live* (Yorkshire TV); *The Bill* (Thames); *Coronation Street*, *Sherlock Holmes*, *In Suspicious Circumstances* and *Celebration* (Granada)

Radio: *The Secret of Fire*, *Joseph Andrews*; *Effie Briest*; *Like They've Never Been Gone*, *Letters To Mam* and *Missing*; all for Radio 4.

Paul Barnhill
Leyton

Born: Knutsford

Trained: East 15

For Birmingham Repertory Theatre:
Julius Caesar, Christian in *The Whisper of Angels Wings*

Theatre: *Shakespeare's Stage* (Shaw Theatre, UK Tour); title role in *Tom Jones* (Theatre Clwyd/UK Tour); title role in *Hamlet* (Beargardens, South Bank and RNT Studio); *Taking Liberties* (Chester Gateway); Bertram in *All's Well That Ends Well*, *Small Box Psychosis* (Nuffield Theatre, Southampton); *Twelfth Night* (RSC UK tour and Vienna); *A Pair of Blue Eyes* (Edinburgh Assembly Rooms); *Romeo & Juliet*, *Anthony & Cleopatra* (Northern Broadsides UK Tours). Opera includes: Frosch in *Die Fledermaus* (Sadlers Wells, UK tour); Mars in *Orpheus in The Underworld* (UK tour D'Oyly Carte); *Pirates of Penzance* (Queens Theatre, London)

TV: *Peak Practice* (Carlton)

Film: *Anorak of Fire* (BBC Screenplay); Gus Flagstone in Mike Leigh's new film *Topsy Turvy*.

Radio: *Friends of Oscar*; *Baby Blue* (Radio 4)

Writing: Writing and acting in 6 part comedy drama *Beyond The Pole* for BBC Radio.

Will Barton
Reg

Born: Vale of Health

Trained: Arts Educational

First appearance for Birmingham Repertory Theatre

Theatre: *Elton John's Glasses* (Queens, West End); *The Visit* (Chichester Festival Theatre); *The Merry Wives of Windsor*, *Women of Troy* (Royal National Theatre); *Angry Old Men* (Plymouth Theatre Royal); *Neville Southall's Washbag* (Finborough); *The Man Outside* (Chelsea Centre); *Webster* (Old Red Lion); *Pioneers in Ingolstadt*, *Purgatory* (Gate); *The Ragged Trousered Philanthropists* (Sheffield Crucible)

TV: *How Do You Want Me?* (2 Series) *Murder Most Horrid*, *The Nicholas Craig Masterclass Series*, *Doctor Who* (BBC); *Jack & The Beanstalk* (LWT), *Barking, Get a Grip on Sex* (Channel 4); *The Bill* (Thames); *Space Precinct* (Mentorn)

Film: *Oscar & Lucinda*

Radio: Co-host and writer of the *Maurice & Barnstaple Show* (Talk Radio); *Burdulane*, *Pioneers in Ingolstadt* (Radio 4).

Lucy Briers
Margot

Trained: Bristol Old Vic Theatre School

For Birmingham Repertory Theatre: Jean Rice in *The Entertainer* and ensemble in *Syme*

Theatre: Desdemona in *Othello* (New Victoria Theatre, Stoke On Trent); Jane Fairfax in *Emma* (Edinburgh Festival); Lady Percy and Doll Tearsheet in *Henry IV* Parts I & II (National Tour and Old Vic for English Touring Theatre); Miranda in *The Tempest* (Salisbury Playhouse); Rosaura in *The Venetian Twins* (Oxford Stage Company); Lucy in *The Rivals* (Nottingham Playhouse); Liddy and Fanny Robbin in *Far From the Madding Crowd* (Worcester)

TV: *Imogen's Face* & *The Ten Percenters* (ITV); *Wives and Daughters*, *Dangerfield*, *Game On*, *Unfinished Business*, *Casualty*, *Pride and Prejudice*, *Screaming*, *The Brittas Empire*, *Red Dwarf*, *A Masculine Ending* (BBC); *The Bill* (Thames TV); *Only You* (Yorkshire TV); *Unnatural Causes* (Anglia TV); *Blackheath Poisonings* (Central TV)

Radio: *The Last of the Barsetshire Chronicles* (BBC Radio); *Henry IV* Parts I & II (World Service)

Paul Bradley
Oliver

Born: Nuneaton
Trained: Manchester University

First Appearance for Birmingham Repertory Theatre

Theatre: Cameo roles at the National Theatre, and Royal Exchange, Manchester. Seasons at Contact Theatre, Manchester; Einstein in *Life of Einstein* (Duke's Playhouse, Lancaster); Truffaldino in *Servant of Two Masters* (Liverpool Playhouse); Fancourt Babberley in *Charley's Aunt* (York Theatre Royal,); Luigi in *Can't Pay? Won't Pay!* (Contact Theatre, Manchester, Crucible, Sheffield); Dogberry in *Much Ado About Nothing* (Nuffield Theatre, Southampton); Feste in *Twelfth Night* (Regent's Park); Benvolio in *Romeo and Juliet* (The Young Vic); Grumio in *Taming of the Shrew* (British Actors Theatre Company). Pantomimes at Theatre Royal Bath, Hackney Empire and Ashcroft Theatre Croydon.

TV includes: Chen in *Red Dwarf*, Burglar in *Bottom*, Warlock and other characters in *The Young Ones* (BBC); *Stop That Laughing at the Back*, *Kate Robbins Show*, Bradley – a devised and co-written children's show (Granada TV). *Don Quixote*, *Conference of the Birds* (Channel Four animated films); Doctor in *C.U Burn in Gaelic* (T na G). Also *Hale & Pace*, *Smith & Jones*, *The Geeks*, *The Bill*, *Boon*, *Murder Most Horrid*. Nigel in *Eastenders* for five years, voted "Most Missed Soap Character" by Readers of Inside Soap Magazine.

Radio: *Supermarket Kisses*, *Love Pray and Do the Dishes*, *Something to Think About* (BBC).

For over ten years Paul has been a member of the band The hKippers, they have released a C.D called *Gutted* and are trying to release another.

Anthony Clark
Director

Since joining Birmingham Repertory Theatre Company in 1990 as an Associate Director, Anthony has directed *The Seagull*, *Of Mice and Men*, *Macbeth*, *Saturday Sunday Monday*, *Cider With Rosie* (national tour), *The Threepenny Opera*, *The Pied Piper*, *My Mother Said I Never Should*, *The Grapes of Wrath*, *The Atheist's Tragedy*, (1994 TMA/Martini Award for Best Director), *The Playboy of the Western World*, *Peter Pan*, *Pygmalion*, *The Red Balloon* (1995 TMA /Martini Award for Best Show for Children and Young People), *The Entertainer*, *Gentlemen Prefer Blondes*, *Pinocchio*, *Julius Caesar*, and new plays: *True Brit, Rough, Playing By the Rules* (Mentorn First Night Production Award), *Nervous Women* and *Syme* (a co-production with the Royal National Theatre Studio). He also directed both *Confidence*, *Down Red Lane* and *Paddy Irishman, Paddy Englishman and Paddy…?* for the first season in The Door.

Anthony graduated from Manchester University Drama Department (RSC Buzz Goodbody Award '79), spent two years directing at the Orange Tree Theatre, London and a year working with Tara Arts before being appointed Artistic Director of Contact Theatre in Manchester in 1984. At Contact Theatre his wide range of productions included new plays: *Face Value*, *Two Wheel Tricycle*, McAlpine's *Fusiliers*, *Green and Homeland*, classics: *Mother Courage and Her Children*, *Blood Wedding*, *A Midsummer Night's Dream*, *The Duchess of Malfi*, *To Kill a Mockingbird* (European premiere - Manchester Evening News Best Production Award 87) and *Oedipus Rex*.

His freelance directing credits include: *Dr Faustus* (Young Vic); *To Kill A Mockingbird* (Greenwich Theatre); *The Snowman* (Leicester Haymarket); *The Red Balloon* (Bristol Old Vic); *The Day After Tomorrow*, *Mother Courage and her Children* and *The Red Balloon* for the Royal National Theatre, and *The Wood Demon* (West End).

As a writer he has had the following plays produced: *Hand it to Them*, *Wake* and a translation of Tolstoy's *The Power of Darkness* at the Orange Tree Theatre, *Tidemark* at the RSC Thoughtcrimes Festival, *A Matter of Life and Death* at the Royal National Theatre, Green and musical adaptations of *The Snowman*, *The Little Prince* and *The Red Balloon* at Contact Theatre in Manchester and *The Pied Piper* and *Pinocchio* at Birmingham Repertory Theatre.

Nettie Edwards
Designer

For Birmingham Repertory Theatre:
Gentlemen Prefer Blondes, The Entertainer,
Awake and Sing!

Theatre includes: *Scary Antics* with
The Shysters (Belgrade Theatre, Coventry);
Simon Black's *Not a Game For Boys*
(Royal Court Theatre Upstairs); tours of
The Tempest and *Henry V* for the Royal
National Theatre's Shakespeare in
Education Project. As Head of Design at
Cheltenham Everyman Theatre: *Macbeth*
(Gold medal winner in the 1995 Prague
Quadrennial); *Death and the Maiden*,
*Les Liaisons Dangereuses, The Sound of
Music*; *Annie, Amadeus, Jane Eyre, All My
Sons, A Doll's House*, T*he Cherry Orchard*,
*A Family Affair, Peter Pan, The Pickwick
Papers, Design for Living, The Mayor of
Casterbridge, A Little Hotel on the Side,
The Provok'd Wife, A View from the Bridge,
Gaslight, The Importance of Being Earnest*.
As Resident Associate Designer at Contact
Theatre in Manchester: *Blood Wedding*
(directed by Anthony Clark and winner of
the Manchester Evening News Award for
Best Design), *Raisin in the Sun*, the world
premiere of *My Mother Said I Never
Should, Antony and Cleopatra* and
The Playboy of the West Indies. At Dukes
Playhouse, Lancaster: *The Winter's Tale,
Jude the Obscure, The Changeling,
The Play of Jennet*. At Everyman Theatre,
Liverpool: *Three Sisters*. At Theatre Royal
York: *The Lucky Chance*. At Gateway
Theatre, Chester: *Torch Song Trilogy*.

TV: Assistant Costume Designer on *By The
Sword Divided*. Nettie was brought up in
Smethwick, and is also a freelance artist
and researcher, and has recently
completed four large scale pieces for
the Royal Caribbean cruise line.

Tim Mitchell
Lighting Designer

Tim is currently lighting designer in
residence at Bimingham Repertory Theatre
where he has lit many productions, these
include:

*The Pajama Game, The Four Alice Bakers,
Paddy Irishman, Paddy Englishman,
Paddy…, Frozen, Whisper of Angels Wings,
The Cherry Orchard, True Brit, Dr Jekyll
and Mr Hyde, Romeo and Juliet,
The Merchant of Venice, Macbeth,
Old Times, Peter Pan* and *The Atheist's
Tragedy* (Gold Medal Winner at the 1995
Prague Quadrennial)

Other productions include: *Romeo and
Juliet* (RSC), *The Red Balloon* and
The Alchemist (Royal National Theatre),
Outside of Heaven, Inventing a New Colour
and *Young Writers Festival* (Royal Court
Theatre); *Someone to Watch Over Me,
When We are Married, Landslide,
The Winslow Boy* and *The Entertainer*
(West Yorkshire Playhouse); *Dead Funny,
Wallflowering* and *Tess of the D'Urbervilles*
(Salisbury Playhouse); *Song at Sunset* and
the *New Directions Season* (Hampstead
Theatre); *Adam Bede, A Passionate
Woman, The Importance of Being Earnest,
Les Liasons Dangereuses* and *Our Boys*
(Derby Playhouse); *A Soldiers Song*
(Theatre Royal Stratford East), *Wodehouse
on Broadway* (BBC TV/Theatre Royal
Plymouth); *As You Like It* and *Anthony and
Cleopatra* (English Shakespeare Company).

The Birmingham RepertoryTheatre Company
Introducing

The Door

Since it was founded in 1913 Birmingham Repertory Theatre Company has been a leading national company. Its programming has introduced a range of new and foreign plays to the British theatre repertoire, and it has been a springboard for many internationally famous actors, designers and directors.

TRIPS TO SEE THE DOLPHINS ENQUIRE WITHIN

Confidence: Jody Watson as Ella, Robin Pirongs as Ben
Photo: Tristram Kenton

As the arts in Birmingham have grown in stature, with the opening of Symphony Hall, the achievements of the City of Birmingham Symphony Orchestra and the arrival of the Birmingham Royal Ballet so there has been massive investment in the resident theatre company. Now the company can present classic, new and discovery plays on a scale appropriate to one of the largest acting spaces in Europe, as well as a consistent programme of new theatre in its studio, by some of the brightest contemporary talent. To celebrate this, the space has a new name and a new look.

The Door's programme seeks to find a young and culturally diverse audience for the theatre, through the production of new work in an intimate, flexible space - work, that reflects, defines and enhances their experience of the world while introducing them to the possibilities of the medium.

Twins: Amelda Brown as Mimi and Anne White as Gigi
Photo: Tristram Kenton

Down Red Lane: Mathew Wait as Spider
Photo: Tristram Kenton

'Birmingham...the workshop of the theatre world."
Michael Billington - The Guardian

New Work at Birmingham Repertory Theatre
- past, present and future

In recent years, Birmingham Repertory Theatre has produced a range of popular, award-winning and critically acclaimed new plays. These include *Divine Right* (1996), Peter Whelan's timely examination of the future of the British monarchy, Debbie Isitt's *Squealing Like a Pig* (1996), Nick Stafford's *The Whisper of Angels' Wings* (1997) and Ayub Khan-Din's *East is East* (1996), a co-production with Tamasha Theatre Company and the Royal Court Theatre, London.

In 1998, Bill Alexander's production of *Frozen* by Bryony Lavery, which starred Anita Dobson, Tom Georgeson and Josie Lawrence, was unaminously praised for its bravery, humanity and humour in exploring the intertwined experiences of a mother, the murderer of her daughter and the psychiatrist who treats him. *Frozen* went on to win the 1998 TMA Barclays Theatre Award for Best New Play and the Central Television Eileen Anderson Award.

In the Autumn, thanks to funding from the Arts Council's Stabilisation Scheme, we were able to start programming our former studio space – now renamed The Door – with a year round programme of new work. Opening with the appropriately named *Confidence* by Judy Upton and followed by Maureen Lawrence's *Twins* and Kate Dean's *Down Red Lane*, the theatre aims to provide a challenging, entertaining and diverse season of ten new plays, including two that tour to arts centres and community venues in the West Midlands.

In support of this work the theatre also

Confidence: Jody Watson as Ella, Robin Pirongs as Ben, Zoot Lynam as Dean.   Photo: Tristram Kenton

runs an extensive education and development programme. Two of the plays in this season: Declan Croghan's *Paddy Irishman, Paddy Englishman and Paddy...?* and *Trips* by Sarah Woods started life on the theatre's attachment scheme for writers. Beginning with just an outline or initial idea for a play, the writer works together with other professional practitioners including actors, directors and designers at appropriate stages throughout the writing process, with the ultimate goal a production of the play at this theatre.

Also in the Autumn, the Education and Literary Departments worked together to present *Transmissions*, a project in which young people from across the city of Birmingham, and from the ages of 7 - 25 wrote and presented their own plays with the support of professional playwrights, directors and actors. If you would like more information on this or other aspects of our work, please contact us on

Tel: 0121 236 6771 x 2108/2109

Ben Payne Literary Manager

The Birmingham Repertory Theatre gratefully acknowledges the support of the Sir Barry Jackson Trust in its new work development programme

From Page to Stage

An opportunity for students to participate in the process of putting on a season of new plays. Access to the country's most contemporary theatre writers, and a chance to work with directors, actors and qualified teachers in exploring a season of cutting edge theatre - Fraser Grace's PERPETUA and Paul Lucas' ALL THAT TROUBLE THAT WE HAD.

What's On Offer?

Workshops

On making block bookings, two workshops will be offered. The first involves an exploration of the content of the text; themes and structure etc. to be led by the Rep's Education Department and held at your college. The second will be run by a writer and the Rep's Associate Director Anthony Clark, and will explore ideas behind the writing and the process of producing the piece from page to stage. These second workshops will take place at the theatre.

After Darks

You can choose to come to the shows which are followed by an After Dark (although you are free to choose when you want to come). This is an opportunity to get the performer's perspective first hand, and to capitalise on that immediate response ensuring that your students get the most out of their time at the theatre.

Scripts

Scripts will be published for each play in a programme format. This provides an opportunity for further study of the text's form and content. Each student has their own copy of each play, at the equivalent of just £1.00. (These texts retail at £6.99).

Discounted Tickets

Tickets are available at the equivalent of just £3 per performance. With tickets normally at £9/£7, this represents a huge discount.

Unbeatable Value

Tickets for all three shows, scripts for each student, workshops with directors, writers and teachers and aftershow discussions with the company are included in the price. Stage to Page is a pro-active approach to serve mutual needs. An opportunity to tackle your curriculum in a unique, accessible way. Suitable for students of Culture, Theatre Arts, English etc.
The complete package works out at only £15 (minimum 15 students, no maximum).

What previous participants have said:
'My students don't usually have access to a professional director. It's brilliant'
'This has been the best part of the course for these students…I'm bowled over by the response. Terrific.'
'I really got to understand how complicated it is…I was much more into it because I'd read it…It was great'

For further details or to book please contact Rachel Gartside, Head of Education on 0121 236 6771

Transmissions: young playwrights

Communication, engagement and the start of something new

As Birmingham's only venue dedicated entirely to new writing, The Door is investing in writers of the future. In Autumn 1998 we launched the first part of our project with plays written by 7-25 year olds with staged readings and performances in our new writing house The Door. Short plays were developed in primary schools and through the Rep's young people's playwriting groups, led by professional writers and directors.

Those taking part in **Transmissions** explored writing, speaking, acting and reading their work with the guidance of professionals at every stage in the process. They developed their imaginative and technical skills in creating stories from action, speech and character.

In December the workshops culminated in a festival of performances. Examples of the extracts and scenes we presented include: *Wish you were here* by Modessor Rashid about a man's past returning to haunt him following his release from prison; Adam Godwin's *The Shop* which centred on the conflict of creativity and responsibility; and *Crossroads* by Sharlene Ferguson in which the friendship between two young women is placed on the line following a night on the town and an unexpected revelation. In all we presented twenty-eight pieces of writing over a two week period.

Photos: Alan Wood

There will be further **Transmissions** projects, including the continuation of the Rep's young playwrights' group, which is now entering its third year. Many young playwrights from this group have gone on to develop their writing through higher education courses such as Theatre Arts or Drama at University.

'I learnt a lot about the hard work that is put into writing a play' VINETA JAIN, SWANSHURST SCHOOL

'Helpful encouraging, insightful, inspiring' TIM JEFFRIES, YOUNG WRITER

'Thank you for the chance to work with some inspiring young people' MAYA CHOWDHRY, WRITER

'Young writers were exposed to a lot of talented professionals, inspired and encouraged to work and to believe in themselves. A lot of young people from the local community benefited.' (THERSA HESKINS, FREELANCE DIRECTOR).

'The festival has given me practical tools to write my plays' ADAM GODWIN, YOUNG WRITER

For more information please contact; Rachel Gartside / Liz Ingrams on 0121 236 6771 ext 2142/2104

What previous participants have said:

'Shy children came out of themselves and they all contributed to the script. Children and parents thoroughly enjoyed the whole experience' TEACHER

Paul Lucas
All That Trouble That We Had

faber and faber

First published in 1999
by Faber and Faber Limited
3 Queen Square, London WC1N 3AU

Typeset by Country Setting, Kingsdown, Kent CT14 8ES
Printed in England by Intype London Ltd

A CIP record for this book
is available from the British Library

ISBN 0–571–20267–5

2 4 6 8 10 9 7 5 3 1

For Ian

Characters

Hannah

Vaughan, Hannah's father

Leyton

Reg, Leyton's brother

Margot, a postwoman

Oliver, a salesman

Act One

SCENE ONE

Vaughan's kitchen. Almost bare, dominated by a large window. As the lights come up, Vaughan is pouring boiling water into two mugs, whilst Hannah peers out of the window. Vaughan crosses to her and hands her the mug.

Hannah Thanks, Daddy.

Vaughan Any change?

Hannah No.

Vaughan sighs, and sits at the table with his mug.

Vaughan I think the waiting is the worst part. The old something-about-to-happen bit, the will-it-won't-it gap with the long, long length and the slow, slow pace. It's very uneventful torture, Princess. I just loathe all the waiting.

Short silence.

Hannah I'm like that with owls.

Vaughan (*nodding*) . . . Mm . . . mm . . .

Hannah I can't abide owls. (*She shivers with immeasurable dread. Sips from her mug. Turns from the window. Smacking lips*) What's this?

Vaughan Mushroom tea I call it.

Hannah Lovely. Seems to be mostly hot water with a mushroom floating in it.

Vaughan Surprisingly tasty, isn't it?

Hannah Where's *your* mushroom?

Vaughan That was the last one.

Hannah So what are you drinking?

Vaughan Mock mushroom tea. Surprisingly tasty.

Hannah Here. (*She takes the mushroom out of her mug and puts it into his.*)

Vaughan Oh no really – Well that's very kind. I'm not sure I deserve you, Hannah, I half live in fear you'll come to your senses one day.

Hannah Don't be silly, I'm fine.

Vaughan You'd tell me if you were gloomy?

Hannah Of course I would. I'd have to work up to it though, I probably couldn't come straight out with it like some people could.

Vaughan Some people are like that, aren't they, yes . . . direct . . .

Hannah What's he doing now?

Vaughan Mr Red Shoes?

Vaughan picks up a telescope and looks out of the window.

Still just sitting there. A harsher mind would ask what he thinks he's messing about at?

He turns back from the window, puts down the telescope.

Hannah It's a nice place to jump from, Daddy, it's the most popular bridge in the country if you're in that sort of mood. He's most likely trying to pluck up courage.

Vaughan If he's not going to do it he might want to consider moving along, he could be holding up genuine

6

depressives. Maybe with fat wallets that we can pop down and get off them in order to pay for . . . What Has To Be Paid For. Look at the time, you-know-who will be calling by soon.

Hannah has picked up the telescope and is looking out of the window.

Hannah Daddy he's stood up!

Vaughan Yes?

Hannah Yes! I think he's going to jump.

She hands Vaughan the telescope.

Vaughan Let's not get over-excited, he might just've got pins and needles . . .

Vaughan looks through the telescope.

No, he looks quite broken, he's got his head in his hands and we might be in for something here, Sweets . . .

Hannah Oh it's a tragic waste but please let it happen, please, please, please, please, please . . .

Vaughan Looking teary and sincere and stepping slowly back, measured paces, working out his run-up . . .

Hannah (*to herself*) Jump-jump-jump-jump-jump . . .

Vaughan Here he goes! Here he goes, he's going, he's going –

Short silence.

Hannah What? Daddy, what?

Vaughan turns back, lowers telescope.

Vaughan He tripped. Just before the edge, he tripped. Backwards.

Hannah Maybe he'll go again.

Vaughan (*sighs*) Maybe.

Vaughan turns back to the window, looks through the telescope.

No. He's running around in circles, or, or, let's say ellipses and he's banging himself about the head . . . and now he is . . . sinking to his knees. Well away from the railings. He is sinking to, of all things, his knees.

Vaughan turns back. Sees that Hannah is close to tears so he puts his arm around her.

Hannah It's hard, Daddy, all this trouble that we're having . . . and I really think we need a hand . . .

Vaughan We'll manage, it'll be over before you know it. It'll be 'all that trouble that we *had*' one day soon. And everything we're having to do at the moment will've been worth it.

Hannah Yes I don't think we're bad people, really, just a little misguided.

Vaughan A touch desperate, that's all.

Hannah I think our hearts are in the right places, we're just . . . making hard choices.

Vaughan There's no malice in us for instance. But without some sort of funds . . .

Hannah Hmmm . . . there's no question of phoning the police, Daddy, even now?

Vaughan No! No, Sweets. Not to put too fine a point on it, that's a mad suggestion. No it's too risky, it's . . . no. Not with what's at stake, we'll manage.

Hannah We will manage, won't we . . .

Vaughan Of course we will, just fine is how we'll manage . . . What's there to cry about?

Hannah . . . No police . . .

Vaughan No police. You and I and no-one else. Like it's been ever since your mother – (*Short silence.*) And when haven't we managed?

Hannah Never.

They embrace warmly.

Daddy, footsteps.

Vaughan Yes, he's here. Let's be dry-eyed, eh?

Vaughan goes to a dresser and takes a roll of bank notes from a jar. There is a knock at the door. Hannah opens it. Leyton enters.

Leyton Hi there.

Hannah ignores him.

I said 'Hi there'.

Hannah Yes. I was ignoring you though.

Leyton I get it, right. It's a bit fucking rude of you, but what the hell. (*to Vaughan*) Is that for me?

Vaughan Yes.

Vaughan hands him the roll of bank notes.

Leyton Thanks.

Leyton starts to count the money. Looks up at Hannah.

See, 'Thanks'. Manners . . . Eighty-five, ninety, ninety-five . . . Ninety-five. What's this, ninety-five?

Vaughan (*clears throat*) We don't have any more.

Leyton Ninety fucking five?

Vaughan We wondered if we could possibly give you a hundred and five the next time.

Leyton Is this a joke?

Vaughan No, if it's anything it's poverty.

Hannah We did everything we possibly could, so if it's not enough well that's too bad.

Vaughan It really has been a struggle, Hannah's right – although her tone's a bit offish.

Leyton Jesus this fucking country, why can't anyone just do what they say they're going to do, we said a hundred, a hundred for each packet and now here we are with this situation. With this ninety-five, pay-you-a-hundred-and-five-next-time situation.

Vaughan We'd be very grateful. It's just we're intellectuals, you see, our work is thought and our wage is inspiration. On top of which, we were one plum short of a tenner on the scratchcards.

Hannah Take it or leave it.

Vaughan No, she doesn't mean that, no. She isn't rude, just spirited.

Leyton Jesus, you crazy harpy. Women. (*to Vaughan*) Their bicycles don't have crossbars, they're a different species, women.

Vaughan A hundred and five next time, no quibbles.

Leyton hands Vaughan a packet.

Leyton A hundred and ten next time.

Hannah That's not fair. You're not a real man, you're dastardly.

Leyton I don't have to take this shit you know. I could walk out of this door here and just never come back, how would that suit you?

Vaughan We wouldn't want you to do that, neither of us.

Leyton You don't have to say I'm dastardly, do you, bit of fucking common courtesy. I'm starting to dread coming here 'cause of you, I have to count to ten before I knock the door.

Hannah Good then, you dastard.

Vaughan She's a live wire, this one, just like her mother.

Leyton You're riddles, you women, lovely fucking curvey riddles. (*to Vaughan*) A hundred and ten the next time and then it's back to a hundred a packet.

Vaughan Right.

Leyton No more messing about with the prices, a hundred a fucking packet, we're all clear and there's no confusion.

Vaughan A hundred a packet.

Leyton Right. And no police.

Vaughan No, no police.

Leyton Good. Well, you two have a nice day now.

Vaughan Thank you.

Leyton waits for a response from Hannah but she pointedly ignores him. He throws his hands up in exasperation.

Leyton Jesus – I mean – Fucking women.

Exits, shaking his head. Hannah closes the door. Vaughan sinks down into a chair, head in one hand.

Vaughan You know you really shouldn't antagonise the man, Hannah, there's no telling what he might do to your mother.

Hannah He shouldn't be able to do this to us. At all.

Vaughan No, but we're managing and all that matters is we get her back here with us isn't it, safe and sound.

Hannah Of course it is Daddy, he's hateful is all.

Vaughan Soon be over, Princess, try and hold on. Just think, when he goes to hell, we'll be able to stand there and smell him melt.

Vaughan pats her hand softly. She responds by putting her other hand on his shoulder. After a moment or two, the sound of a distant splash. Vaughan gets to his feet hurriedly, picks up the telescope and looks out of the window.

Hannah What was that?

Vaughan He's jumped! Mr Red Shoes! He's done it!

Vaughan Quickly! Quickly!

Vaughan pulls from behind the door a pair of thigh-length waders, which he then struggles into. Hannah meanwhile opens a cupboard and takes out a large net, which she hands to Vaughan.

Hannah Be careful, Daddy.

Vaughan hurries out.

Careful.

Hannah picks up the packet and looks at it. Puts it down, carefully. Then she sits, and begins to pray. Lights fade.

Reg's lounge. Vinyl records everywhere. Music, and Reg is dancing – ineptly some would say – to it. Leyton enters, with a bottle in his hand. He watches Reg for a moment, until Reg finally notices him, stops dancing and turns off the music.

Leyton Fucking . . . Reg, did you exceed the stated dose of something? Jesus . . . I've never seen anyone else in the world dance like that, Reg, not even at weddings . . .

Reg Sorry, I was a slave to the rhythm . . . got a new record yesterday . . .

Leyton pours himself a drink.

Leyton What do you mean 'new'? One you actually haven't got already?

Reg Well no, a new copy. Of the Silly Little Fridges L.P. I mean I've got other copies, but this is a promo, not a scratch on it either.

Reg holds the record up to the light to check, then puts it in its sleeve.

Leyton Jesus, like you don't have enough copies of Denzil fucking Golden. How many's that now, a hundred of each?

Reg Well, it's a collection, Leyton.

Reg opens a drawer, which slides out like a drawer in a mortuary. It's full of records. He puts his new one in it and closes it.

Leyton You're like an addict or something.

Reg Now that's a bit rich, isn't it, you standing there pouring yourself a drink at this hour and calling me an addict. They've shown it beyond doubt you know, Leyton, that stuff you're drinking it kills brain cells, no two ways about it.

Leyton Well, sometimes those bastard brain cells have it coming. Sometimes you've got to kill those fuckers in self-defence.

Reg You see that's just crazy talk.

Leyton Here.

Throws him a bundle of notes.

Here's your share from this morning. Buy yourself another record.

Reg Thanks Leyton.

Leyton Count it if you want.

Reg No, God, I don't need to count it, don't be silly.

Leyton It's ten pounds short, they only gave me eighty.

Reg Right, only . . . I can't say I approve of this thing that we're doing . . . I can't help feeling it's going to catch up with us, y'know . . .

Leyton You're happy enough to take the money, Reg, that's a bit fucking hypocritical to start disapproving now.

Reg Well I'm not saying I'm a saint, I may even be on shaky ground in a, what would you call it, a moral grey area, but the thing is I'm not happy about it. Having that woman in the house is making me jumpy.

Leyton Where is she anyway?

Reg I left her out in the garden.

Leyton *What?* You did *what?* (*He leaps to his feet in disbelief.*) Jesus you crazy bastard, left her in the – Jesus!

Leyton exits hurriedly. After a while he returns with an urn.

Reg (*while Leyton is off*) She's only been there a minute or two, Leyton. (*Beat.*) I couldn't enjoy the music with her in here.

Leyton re-enters. Plonks urn on the table.

Leyton There was a fucking slug on her. Left her in the garden, a fucking magpie could've nabbed her.

Reg That's just a weird thing to think of, Leyton, that's a boozy idea to mention.

Leyton Magpies steal stuff, everyone knows – Look, just let's keep her in this fucking room from now on. Where we can see her.

Reg Let's give her back, eh? We've made a good bit of money now. Paid off all our debts. Eh Leyton? I mean I've got a say in this, haven't I? It was me that found the urn wasn't it?

Leyton And whose idea was it to make money out of it?

Reg Well, yours of course. But then the address and everything was on the thing, it didn't need much work to find the owners – anyway, what I'm saying is, it's not just the ethics, it's the supernatural aspect that's making me have second thoughts.

Leyton Is this another thing about spooks?

Reg Let's not say 'spooks' Leyton, let's say 'forces'. I mean, I'm no fan of religion, you know that, well religion's been responsible for some of the worst wars and marriages in the world, but I sometimes think there's got to be *something*. *Something* after this. It wouldn't make sense otherwise.

Leyton Who say's it gotta make sense? Look, you don't want to take the money, fine.

Leyton puts out hand for money. Reg doesn't return it.

Reg I didn't exactly say that, Leyton . . . you know I'm short right now . . . these records cost an arm and a leg . . .

Leyton I'll come and visit you, when you're sat there in Our Lady's Home For Elderly Twats And Misfits. Dribbling away next to the traffic wardens and the morris dancers. Estate agents and football referees for company. And you know what colour the walls are going to be, Reg? Moral Grey.

Reg I don't want *that*, Leyton, that's no future, I want to get a career that's of use to society. Maybe even be someone who saves people's lives, like a heart surgeon or a television repair man.

Leyton That's absolutely beautiful, you do that Reg.

Reg I'm just saying I hope you do that too. Use this money to get yourself started in something.

Leyton I told you, I'm going to open a club.

Reg With women wrestlers?

Leyton Yeah.

Reg Well that's nice, good. 'Cause I'm your older brother, I'm supposed to steer you away from . . . immoral things.

Leyton Jesus I'm twenty-five Reg. I don't need any fucking steering.

Reg You know you could moderate your language a little too.

Leyton Jesus Christ . . . I'm twenty fucking five and look at the shit I get . . . Listen, I've done my time in crappy jobs, and it's a mug's game. First sign of trouble they kicked us out of that factory like dogs. After all the weeks of service we gave Dark Satanic Mills plc, building those stupid kiddies' playground products.

Reg There was a sudden slide in the market for swings and roundabouts, it was no-one's fault.

Leyton And we walk straight out of the factory and what's the first thing we come across? This urn. I'm not going to look that gift horse in the mouth, Reg. I'm not going to be still sat in this dump when I'm an old man with enormous ears. Those great big enormous ears old men get . . . argh! . . . urgh! Jesus!

> *Leyton spins in circles clutching his ear-lobes as if possessed. A knock at the door.*

Now what? Who's that?

Reg Just Margot probably.

> *Reg opens the door. It is indeed Margot, the post-woman. Leyton begins to smooth his hair, brush down his jacket etc . . . Puts on shades.*

Margot Howdy Reg, sorry I'm so late again.

Reg Margot, hi – I said, didn't I, it's Margot.

> *Margot enters and sits down.*

Leyton Hi there.

Margot Hello Mr Grayson.

Leyton Leyton.

Margot (*to Reg*) I was up 'til four again photographing my resident hedgehog. Reverie's going to get me fired. Here.

> *She hands him a record-sized packet from her postbag.*

Reg Thanks, great.

Leyton Anything for me in there?

Margot Sorry, no.

Reg This is another Mobile Home-icide E.P., great.

Leyton I was kind of expecting my *Motiveless Crimes* today. There's a pull-out on horse mutilaters this month.

Margot Not here, sorry. (*to Reg*) Would you like a pamphlet?

Reg Pamphlet?

Margot They're free.

Reg Would I ever.

Margot It's all about the bridge.

Reg Corp's bridge?

Margot I'd rather call it The Bridge Designed By William Corp. He was my great-uncle, you know.

Reg I think you said, that's great. Designed a bridge, that's a real achievement.

Margot It's the only example of his work left standing. Nine bridges and two lighthouses he designed and this is the only one standing and we've got it right here.

Leyton I'll take one of those, I'm mad about bridges.

Margot Great.

She gives him a pamphlet.

Leyton I've, er, I've got a little whatsit thing here for you too. A gift.

He hands her a box of chocolates.

Margot Another one? Thanks. Chocolates. (*Looks at them.*) Oh. That's a lovely thought Mr Grayson, but you know, I have a violent dislike of praline, so . . .

She hands the box back.

Leyton Fuck.

Margot But I'd like to say a big Thank You anyway. (*to Reg*) Yeah, it's a shame because that bridge is a work of art and what do people do? They throw themselves off it. Every other day someone goes up there and jumps off the thing. The only known example of his work and it's hup! Can't take any more, excuse me, hup! and over. Regrettable.

Reg So you're what, you're trying to raise awareness with this pamphlet thing.

Margot Raise awareness, that's a lovely way of putting it Reg.

Leyton I nearly got you flowers.

Margot I appreciate the gesture.

Leyton I always seem to fuck up with this kind of thing.

Margot You weren't to know. But I'd appreciate it if you could stop mentally undressing me now.

Leyton . . . Shit, you can tell that kind of thing?

Reg So what happened to all the other bridges, Margot?

Margot Fell down mostly. Tricky things to get right, bridges. It takes practice to design a good one.

Leyton . . . Shit that's what then, intuition or something?

Margot It was commissioned by a wealthy landowner to join two communities together and shorten the walk to his favourite pub. Not for people to jump to their certain deaths from. Hey, the sight of roses at dusk, that's worth hanging around for, you and I'd say – not to these people though. They're over the side roses or no roses.

Leyton Would roses be a good idea? A bunch of roses?

Margot Oh I like my roses wild, Mr Grayson. I always think picked flowers are dying flowers and have an ineffable sadness about them, it's just how it seems to me.

Leyton Fuck. I give up then.

Margot This life can thrill you giddy but you watch that bridge for any length of time and someone'll be up there toying with a dark idea. Ah well, work to do, running late.

She starts to leave.

See you again tomorrow, no doubt. If I don't take a sickie. Swwwww . . . fog hanging in gardens, that just came into my head now, lovely . . .

She's gone. Reg closes the door after her.

Leyton Jesus. How d'you . . . converse like that?

Reg Hm? I don't know. I just . . . Are these chocolates going spare?

Leyton (*sighs*) Yeah. Help yourself.

Hands Reg chocolates, which he tucks into. Also examines his new record. Leyton takes off shades and sits.

Jesus . . . I swear I'm missing something . . . I mean I like women, I really, really like women, but I never seem to be able to find out what makes them tick. Or to hug them.

Reg Baked apples, Dad always said.

Leyton What? Dad said that?

Reg Uh-huh. If you want to seduce a woman, Reg:

baked apples. That was Dad's advice. (*munching*)
Mmmmmm . . . liqueur . . .

Leyton Hm. I mean I do okay, I get my share, but never
. . . I mean, I'm well into double figures . . .

Reg You're not counting in Roman numerals now are
you?

Leyton What?

Reg Nothing.

Leyton Roman numerals?

Reg It was just a joke, I was making light of things.

Leyton Shit. Maybe that's it. No sense of humour,
maybe I should get one of those fuckers, women giggle
all the time don't they . . . I'm fed up paying for it. I'm
always paying for it. I want a bit of tenderness, that kind
of stuff, a bit of caressing and playing footsie and talking
in that baby talk, saying 'snookums' or 'cutie-pie' or –

Reg Leyton, you're making my toes curl.

Leyton I swear all you bastards are giving out signals
I don't know about. I reckon you click to each other like
bats. Fucking high-pitched clicking I can't hear.

Reg You mind if I put this on?

*He's putting his new record on. Leyton gets up and
starts to exit.*

Leyton Oh fuck. You're driving me nuts with that stuff.

Reg It's live from Builth Wells, Leyton. From his 1989
Wales and the Isle Of Man tour.

Leyton This is no way to fucking live. (*He checks his
ears in a mirror, pulls at the lobes, etc. Grimaces.*) No
dancing, alright? You dance like that yet she talks to you
more than she does to me, what a fucking riddle . . .

Exits. The music starts. Reg slowly starts to move a little bit, then more and more. Leyton comes back in.

No fucking dancing. Jesus.

Reg stops. Leyton exits again. Lights fade and music comes up.

SCENE THREE

Vaughan's kitchen. Vaughan enters, dragging a body (which should have red shoes). Hannah goes to help him.

Hannah Careful of your back, Daddy.

Vaughan (*breathless*) Heavy man.

Hannah Perhaps he had a thyroid problem. That might've been why he was unhappy. Or it might've been something else altogether.

Vaughan begins rifling through the dead man's pockets. Finds a wallet, which he hands to Hannah. Then he returns to his rifling.

(*looking in wallet*) Not a lot here, Daddy. A five pound note.

Vaughan Every little helps.

Hannah A supermarket loyalty card. (*She reads it.*) Thomas Schwartz.

Vaughan Here.

Hands her a bun he's taken from the body's pocket.

Hannah A Chelsea bun.

Vaughan He mustn't've fancied it.

Hannah Lost his appetite, bless him.

Hannah takes a bite from the bun, then hands it back to Vaughan. He meanwhile takes a small book from the jacket pocket of the body.

Vaughan Collected Works of Sylvia Plath . . .

He hands Hannah a piece of paper taken from inside the book.

Vaughan A note.

Hannah (*reading*) 'Dear Bastard World, This poisoned gap between being unborn and dead is getting on my tits besides I am no-one's Dream Man it turns out and bloody lonely. P.T.O. – (*She turns note over and continues to read.*) – The price of fags also. Good night you cruel men especially. P.S. Bastards.'

She carefully folds the note back up and hands it back to Vaughan who puts it back where he found it.

The poor love. He must've been feeling very very sad.

Vaughan Hm. Must have.

Hannah He probably felt he was on the margins.

Vaughan The margins, yes. (*stopping searching*) That's it. Nothing else.

Hannah Well, five pounds is five pounds Daddy.

Vaughan Not to underestimate that, and accepting your point and the way you're looking at things there, Sweets, none the less we really do need a bit more than that. A hundred and ten pounds is bordering on a tall order.

Vaughan is now looking inside the body's mouth.

Now then. He does possess a gold tooth.

Hannah (*a bit horrified*) Oh Daddy. Daddy, no.

They look at each other. Hannah bites her lip.

Vaughan The thing is, we're not bad people in the slightest.

Hannah slowly goes and takes a tool-box from under the sink, and hands it to Vaughan. He takes out some pliers and begins clumsily extracting the tooth.

Hannah (*quietly*) We have our reasons, we have our reasons . . .

Vaughan Anyone would do the same in our position, and even if they wouldn't, so what?

Hannah So what anyway. That's them Daddy. So what. We love Mummy, that's all.

Much cracking and banging as Vaughan struggles with the tooth.

He's young. It's nearly always the young, have you noticed?

Vaughan Yes, well, there's not much point if you're in your eighties, is there? I think I need the – ah! –

Vaughan takes a hammer from the toolbox and begins bashing the face of the corpse with it. Then he puts the hammer down and goes to work with the pliers again.

It'll be worth it soon. When we get your mother back.

Hannah We'll have a party for ourselves then, won't we? Out in the yard.

Vaughan Presuming it's sunny.

Hannah Yes. Not a wild one like the ones Mummy used to go to that lasted a fortnight and were always being broken up by the police.

Vaughan Well, your mother needed to stay out longer than most people because she had so many friends, that's all. (*sighs*) I suppose it was silly of me to carry the urn around with me like that. It was bound to end in disaster.

Hannah Well I did say, Daddy. I said 'I know you miss her but I'm not sure this can be helping either of you.'

Vaughan She was always so active, I thought she might like to revisit all her favourite places, and do some fun things, maybe go on a roller coaster, but – Aha!

He has extracted the tooth. Hands it to Hannah.

There. We'll need to clean that up a bit.

A knock at the door.

Now then. How's this for a hairy moment, hm. We'd better hide our friend here, hadn't we, in case that's someone who puts two and two together and disapproves.

Hannah Panic stations Daddy, yes.

They open a drawer in the dresser, and it slides out like a mortuary drawer. They dump the body in there and close the drawer. Vaughan gets out of his waders and wipes the blood from his hands. Another, louder knock at the door. This time Hannah answers it. It is Margot.

Margot Howdy. Letter for you.

Hannah Oh. Thank you.

Margot It's recorded delivery so I'll need you to sign.

Hannah Okay then.

She comes inside to get a pen, and Margot follows her in.

Margot (*to Vaughan*) Hello.

Vaughan Hello, not that we've got anything to hide.

Hannah hands letter to Vaughan who opens it.
Hannah signs for the letter. Margot tries to disguise
a yawn.

Margot Excuse me, I was up all night. That's why I'm so late with your post again. Still, just you and Mr Schwartz to go.

Hannah Mr . . . Schwartz . . .?

Hannah picks up the pliers and gently puts them in a drawer.

Margot Yeah. I've shed about half a stone this morning thanks to that man. Look at all these presents and cards I've got to deliver to him.

She shows a few presents etc. from her post-bag.

Margot Oh, would you like a pamphlet, they're free?

Hannah Oh okay, thank you. (*reading*) *The History of the Bridge Designed by William Corp*. It sounds absolutely . . . (*thinks*) factual.

Vaughan We're up to our necks in shit, apparently.

Hannah What d'you mean, Daddy?

Vaughan This is from the bank. It says we're up to our necks in shit.

Margot I'm sure it doesn't use those exact words though.

Vaughan shows Margot the letter.

Oh. They're normally more circumspect.

Vaughan Look at how much we owe, Sweets.

Hands letter to Hannah.

Hannah It's not all that much, look, most of it's noughts.

Margot That's the spirit. Take rainbows, what a treat when the rain's let up, and then all of a sudden the sun's out and: a rainbow. Not much, no, no, just light becoming seven colours, but enough to make you want to take a day off work.

Vaughan They want to take the house.

Hannah It's not worth anything, it's in the worst location in the world, so the Estate Agent said.

Vaughan It says they want to stop us benefiting from any sentimental value it might have. They've also enclosed a breakdown of how much you'd receive in the event of my death as long as it looks like an accident.

Margot This is the most desirable place in the world to live, it's just people don't appreciate the bridge. It's a mecca for the suicidal, yes, but how many people know about its decorative scrollwork? Or even who designed it? There's more to bridges than meets the eye. There's a lot of deciding where to put pillars goes on behind the scenes, it's all in the pamphlet.

Hannah Oh.

Margot They fall down if you're not careful, the pillars have got to be just right. Anti-collapse mechanisms to some extent. I mean look at the thing, the way it casts shadows on the water there, it's like a mid-air cathedral, I could watch the way – Oh shh – ! No, don't do it!

A distant splash.

Brother. Would you believe it, what a snub to the effort that went into those cantilevers, it's as sad as it is annoying.

Vaughan Someone jumped? Just like that?

Hannah Nobody just jumps. They always ponder first.

Vaughan They contemplate to the point of procrastination, it can drive you nuts.

Margot Head first, straight over, didn't even break stride this one. Couldn't wait to sail past the thousands of hours of craftsmanship in the fretted ironwork up there.

Vaughan Just like that . . . Did you notice if he was wearing a watch?

While Margot peers out of the window, Vaughan gets into his waders. Hannah helps him open the drawer and take out the body. He drags it out and closes the door. Dialogue over all this.

Margot When you think of all the work that went into that bridge . . . six months of construction . . . then four years of renovation . . . then more repairs after the damage it suffered in the war . . . Those German bombers nearly did for it, alright. The vibration of them flying over it caused two pillars to collapse. All that work, and then people go and do (*gestures*) that kind of thing. It makes you want to cry . . . and then stop crying, have a quick cigar and get on with it, it really does . . .

Exits. Hannah picks up the letter, and reads it worriedly as the lights fade.

SCENE FOUR

Reg's lounge. Music. Reg is sat at the table, either having convulsions or enjoying the music, it's hard to tell. Leyton is trying to move a spoonful of ash from an urn into a small plastic bag.

Leyton Reg? Reg!

Reg stops his strange movements.

You're going to make me spill it.

Reg gets up and turns off the music.

Reg I find it helps me relax. Takes my mind off things, like what you're doing with that poor woman there, Leyton.

Leyton Okay, but all your jiggling about was going to make me spill this stuff.

Reg Boy oh boy, Leyton, I don't know how you can do that.

Leyton Don't start with this Reg, we've been over it.

Reg It's kidnap pure and simple.

Leyton It's not kidnap, it's just theft.

Reg In my book I've got this down under K for Kidnap.

Leyton You can't kidnap a pot. You can only kidnap something that's alive. A dead thing isn't a person, is it? This is theft. It's not even theft, all I'm doing is accepting a reward from them for returning their lost item.

Reg People *volunteer* a reward, and I don't think these people are volunteering. I mean if they didn't pay you, what would you do?

Leyton I don't know. I'm not even thinking that way. I'll worry about what I'll do if they don't pay when they don't. There's a thousand things I could do. (*Beat.*) I could wank in it.

Reg Oh *mercy* . . .

Leyton What?

Reg Lord in Heaven, Leyton, you're not going to – Holy Mother of God, well that's just plain wrong.

Leyton What the fuck you getting so worked up about? It's just an example.

Reg That's just plain sick, mercy, mercy, mercy.

Leyton What, wanking in an urn is sick now? Since when?

Reg Since always Leyton, that's, that's the worst thing I have ever, in the name of the Lord, Leyton, you carry that kind of stuff around in your head with you?

Leyton What?

Reg You entertain those sorts of ideas all the time?

Leyton What are you saying, Reg, I'm some sort of headcase?

Reg No, but holey moley, Leyton . . .

Leyton I don't hear voices or nothing, I just have ideas, Jesus, it was just an idea alright? One idea out of many, okay if you don't like it, that's just off the top of my head.

Reg Don't like it, it's just plain *wrong* . . .

Leyton Okay! Okay you docile fuck, at least I *have* ideas, you fucking braindead zombie freak!

   Silence.

Reg I don't think braindead's fair.

Leyton I know, you just shouldn't wind me up.

Reg I have lots of ideas.

Leyton I know.

Reg When we worked at the factory, I was known as The Ideas Man, – I was well-known for – The Ideas Man they called me. There goes The Ideas Man they'd say, meaning me.

Leyton Look, you're not a zombie, you just wind me up. All I want is to get out of this place, start again somewhere else. Forget about all the years I've wasted here. Make out it never happened.

Reg I just thought your idea was on the sick side . . .

Leyton Okay, okay, forget the wank idea, I'll do something else if they don't pay. I'll put bubble-gum in it or something. That okay?

Reg Well it's not ideal but it's better than the other thing.

Leyton There we are then, it'll be bubble-gum, plan B . . . B for bubble-gum . . .

Leyton is now pouring himself another drink.

Reg I mean to you it's just ash, but to them it's all that's left.

Leyton I know.

Reg *Bubble gum*'s bad enough I'd say.

Leyton Fine. (*He knocks back his drink.*) I'll go with the *bubble gum* idea.

Lights fade.

SCENE FIVE

Vaughan's kitchen. Vaughan enters, dragging the seemingly dead Oliver.

Vaughan . . . another heavy one . . . big overcoat . . .

Hannah Is that him? The one who jumped Just Like That?

Vaughan begins to search Oliver's pockets, throws out various bits of chalk, string etc . . .

Vaughan Two in one day is something of a lucky break isn't it, Angel . . .

Hannah (*distracted*) . . . Yes . . . He looks serene, doesn't he?

Vaughan He does, which is lovely. Always nasty when their faces get bashed off.

Vaughan holds up a watch he has taken from Oliver's wrist.

Look at this. A gold watch, could be valuable.

Hannah What's that written on the back of his hand?

Vaughan (*reading*) 'Jump'.

Vaughan opens Oliver's overcoat and lets out a cry of surprise.

Hannah What's wrong Daddy?

Vaughan He's a policeman. Look, he's in uniform. A crushed helmet.

Vaughan holds up a very badly crushed helmet.

Hannah That might be a problem for us, mightn't it?

Vaughan I think so. We don't really want to be involving ourselves with the police because although we're only good people gone slightly desperate, rules are rules in some people's eyes.

Hannah Maybe it's best to put him back where you found him.

Vaughan In case he's more trouble than he's worth, yes.

Hannah And, Daddy, I'd put the watch back perhaps.

Vaughan Yes. So there's no question of wrong-doing, good idea. Where did I put it . . .?

Vaughan looks for watch. Oliver groans. Vaughan and Hannah freeze.

Now then. This is unbelievable trouble.

Hannah Sometimes dead people make sounds, for some kind of medical reason that's not strange.

Vaughan Do they, yes.

Hannah It's frightening at first but you get used to it I think. I think I read that somewhere.

Vaughan It would be a relief if you have.

Oliver Am I dead?

Hannah and Vaughan are startled.

Vaughan Do they generally talk?

Hannah I'm just trying to quickly remember but my instinctive answer would be no, never ever.

Oliver sits up and rubs his head.

Oliver . . . uuuuhhhhhh . . .

Vaughan Now here's a talking point.

Oliver . . . Ooooohhh . . . Hello there.

Vaughan Hello.

Oliver Am I . . . deceased?

Vaughan We're just trying to establish that ourselves.

Hannah I, I don't think this can be right.

Vaughan Me neither.

Hannah Because it's a two hundred foot drop from the bridge and who could live after that sort of fall?

Vaughan Nobody at all could.

Oliver Except Lieutenant I. M. Chisov. He's in *The Guinness Book of Records*, fell nearly twenty-two thousand feet, but that was into soft snow.

Hannah Are you a ghost do you think?

Oliver A ghost, ohhhh, I really hope not. That'll involve a lot of hanging around will it, to be honest I'd be better off alive if that's the case.

Hannah Well. Does this hurt?

She kicks his shin.

Oliver Ow! Yes!

Hannah Sorry.

Oliver Yes madam, that hurt like blazes.

Hannah Sorry. But I don't think you can be a ghost, if you feel pain.

Oliver That'll bruise up like nobody's business . . . Well leaping to my death's turned out to be a real waste of time then, huh?

Vaughan Perhaps you'd like to go back up there and jump again, clear things up once and for all? I could keep hold of your watch in the meantime and if you survive the second jump I'll give it straight back?

Oliver My watch, sir?

Vaughan We had our reasons for taking it off you . . .

Vaughan hands Oliver the watch. Oliver looks at it.

Hannah We're not a danger to the public, in fact we're quite bookish.

Oliver Nope, not mine sir. Mine's a digital with a

twenty-four hour clock option, comes in handy. So the man in the shop said. Anyway I keep mine in my inside pocket on account of this curious rash I come out in –

He reaches for his inside pocket and realises for the first time he is wearing a police uniform.

What's this, some kind of fancy dress I'm in, what?

Hannah Did you forget you were in uniform, Officer?

Oliver Officer? (*Looks blankly.*) I expect you've got one of those dark senses of humour everyone goes on about, where taste goes out of the window?

Vaughan You're not a policeman?

Oliver I mean you've already kicked me literally while I was down, you didn't have to dress me up, some people would say that's distasteful given my current mood.

Vaughan Then, then what are you?

Oliver I sell artificial sweeteners.

Vaughan In a police uniform?

Oliver No, in a moleskin suit. Least, I used to. With padded elbows.

Hannah Why are you wearing a uniform at all then?

Oliver This is the first I knew about it. I certainly wasn't wearing this get-up when I jumped.

Vaughan Your clothes can't've changed half way through your fall?

Oliver Well, these clothes don't even fit me, look at them.

Stands up to reveal ludicrously tight uniform. A button pings off the jacket.

It really wasn't you two?

Vaughan No.

Oliver This is a sort of mad underworld, is it, where I get trapped in a loop of weird events for eternity?

Vaughan No, this is England. You can tell by the bruise on your shin.

Oliver (*to Hannah*) You don't know your own strength, madam.

Hannah Sorry.

Vaughan Look, there's the bridge. The bridge you jumped from.

Oliver looks out of the window.

Oliver That's it alright. High, isn't it? Could use a lick of paint too. But that's the bridge, we have a consensus on that.

Vaughan We saw you jump – well the Postmanwoman did – and I went down and fished you out –

Oliver So I would've drowned otherwise, it was you dragging me out that saved my life.

Vaughan Hm, yes, although we don't mind playing that aspect of the story down to tell the truth . . .

Oliver (*looking at watch*) Well now here's a thing. It's got my dad's name on it. Well, his nickname anyway. The Terrier, see? They called him that because he never gave up.

Hannah But that doesn't explain the uniform, or does it?

Oliver Well it doesn't explain that, no, but he *was* a policeman if that gets us anywhere.

Vaughan A bit smaller than you?

Oliver Yes, I know you weren't trying to draw attention to my weight problem, but it's fair to say I'm more of a blob than he was.

Vaughan So you might somehow be wearing your father's uniform?

Oliver Well I can't think how – Dad died of his own accord years ago and I haven't seen this uniform since. But there's a pocket-book in here that . . . yeah, these are notes he made about a serial killer called The Beast UK . . . and this is the artist's impression they did of the guy, I remember 'cause dad used to hang copies all over the house, then draw different wigs and beards on them. It used to scare the pyjamas off me.

Hannah Perhaps you changed into it and just don't remember?

Oliver That's an idea worth entertaining.

Hannah You were in a confused state, after all.

Vaughan This has thrown me a bit, you know, I might need a sit down.

Oliver I'd like to apologise to the two of you for landing you with all of this. This is the thanks you get for saving my life.

Hannah A glass of water, that's what we should all have. A nice sit down and a glass of water.

Oliver I don't want to come across as any kind of freeloader . . .

Hannah Don't be silly.

Hannah pours the three of them a glass of water each.

Oliver Thanks madam.

Hannah Oh, it's Hannah. And this is my father, Vaughan.

Oliver Hannah and Vaughan, how do you do, I'm Oliver Hoff.

Hannah hands Vaughan and Oliver their water.

Vaughan Thanks, Sweets. Glass of water, pwwww.

Hannah You should really get out of those wet and inappropriate clothes, Oliver, but the thing is we've got no spare clothes, or even towels. We've sold everything we own to pay for . . . What Has To Be Paid For.

Oliver Oh, don't worry about me, I'm drying out nicely, thanks.

Hannah So Oliver – No, you probably don't want to talk about it.

Oliver How I came to be jumping?

Hannah Just ignore me.

Oliver That's sort of a long story, Hannah. (*sips*) This water's certainly lovely, thank you. (*sips*) It'll probably bore the pants off you.

Hannah We don't mind.

Oliver I don't have much of a time of it, going from door to door trying to foist artificial sweeteners on people, with total strangers that you wouldn't think have got anything to gain by it calling me 'Lard-Arse' and 'Mr Wobbly' and that kind of thing. Then I'll go to some cheap hotel, one of those places with white and gold wardrobes which always make me think of childrens' coffins, and I'll be sitting there bursting my blisters with a pin and trying to remember not to stand so close to the customers or something, and I can't help wondering why I bother getting up in the morning. When you think how there's foxes and little rabbits that'll chew their own legs off to escape from snares, or there's men like Second

Steward Poon Lim who could hang on to a raft, all alone, for a hundred and thirty-three days – well, life must really be a special thing if you're not stuck being Oliver Hoff. It must be worth all the effort, as long as you're not a lemming, or me.

Short silence.

Vaughan A hundred and thirty three days, that's over four months.

Oliver Poon Lim his name was, one hell of a Second Steward. He's in *The Guinness Book of Records* too. I used to know every record off by heart. I got *The Guinness Book of Records* as a prize at school. Only thing I ever won. For colouring-in. I'm going on, I'll shut up now I promise.

Hannah No, you're not going on all that much.

Oliver It's pretty preposterous that I was ever born, unless the idea is to punish the world. Knowing me, I'll end up doing something unpopular and global. I'm probably incubating an alien egg or something. And I smell.

Hannah You're sensitive, which goes against the grain for men. Daddy's like that, he cries when he notices autumn's arrived.

Vaughan If I'm not careful, yes.

Oliver I don't really cry. (*sips*) Except in my sleep. (*sips*) I have this dream that I'm a child knocking on doors and running away. Rat Tat Ginger we used to call it. And at the end of the dream – and this is the bit that's supposed to be interesting – at the end of the dream I go up to my own door, where I live now, and ring the bell. Great bell, plays five different tunes, the man in the shop threw in the batteries free, but getting to the point: the person who answers the door is me. All grown-up like I am now. And I know it was Me As A Child who rang the bell, but he's run off. He's nowhere to be seen. That's when I wake up, sweating buckets and shouting my head off. And for some reason this dream scares the living daylights out of me. It makes me want to be sick.

Short silence.

Hannah I'm like that with owls. They can turn their heads right round in circles. . . . revolving heads . . . urgh . . .

She shudders.

Oliver Are there a lot of owls around here?

Hannah None, none for miles.

Vaughan That's why she decided to be scared of them rather than of spiders, say. Me, I chose sand-snakes. Very rare in England.

Hannah More water, Oliver?

Oliver Oh, I probably shouldn't . . . I really ought to be getting on.

Hannah Where?

Oliver Where?

Hannah Where will you go?

Oliver Oh . . . to tell you the honest truth, I don't really know.

Vaughan You don't have a home?

Oliver No I don't, Vaughan, I don't, I gave notice on my flat and then I gave all my things to charity. I kind of put all my eggs in one basket, I was gambling on the suicide thing working out, lack of foresight.

Hannah You could stay here.

Oliver Oh no, really. I couldn't. I wouldn't dream of it.

Hannah He could stay with us a while, Daddy.

Vaughan Could he?

Oliver No you've done enough for me already.

Hannah We've got a spare room upstairs.

Oliver Really?

Hannah Yes. It'd be no trouble. Please stay.

Oliver You're absolutely sure . . .?

Hannah Yes. Aren't we, Daddy?

Vaughan Well if you've got something more pressing to attend to, like a second jump for example . . .

Oliver I don't know what to say.

Vaughan I suppose having made the offer it'd be plain rude not to mean a single word of it . . .

Oliver Well that's certainly uncommon kindness, I feel humbled by this.

Vaughan . . . to admit to just being polite and a little mortified you've now accepted.

Oliver I'm genuinely humbled. Thank you, thank you so much.

Hannah (*beaming*) I'll go and put a pillow and a candle in the spare room then.

Oliver I don't believe the level of kindness I'm seeing.

Vaughan Stay, yes. It shouldn't complicate anything. No. Actually, yippee.

Blackout.

SCENE SIX

The bridge. A sign on the bridge reads 'OH COME ON NOW'.
Margot is tying another one next to it which reads 'IT'S
NOT SO BAD'. *Leyton enters.*

Margot Howdy Mr Grayson.

Leyton Er, hi, hi there. It's Leyton.

*Margot finishes tying her signs and stands back to
check they're straight.*

Margot (*gesturing to signs*) What d'you think?

Leyton Er . . .

Leyton leans over and reads them.

Margot Careful there. Gravity kicks in at a certain
point.

Leyton Yeah, great signs. I love 'em, top signs.

Margot Thanks. Well the pamphlet was stage one, and
this is stage two.

Leyton Stage two right. I, er, I got you something. A, er,
token of my, er . . . y'know . . .

He hands her a microwaveable meal.

Margot A microwaveable meal, oh. (*Looks at it.*) Baked
apples, that's really nice of you. I didn't know they did
those. (*reading label*) Part of the 'Friends Are More
Trouble Than They're Worth' range, that's a new one on
me, thanks a lot. But, er, I don't have a microwave.

She hands him back the meal.

Leyton Fuck.

Margot You seem to be spending a lot of money lately, if you don't mind me saying?

Leyton Well, hey, if you've got it you've got to spend it, right?

Margot I just thought with you losing your job and everything . . .

Leyton Money's everywhere, you just got to know where to look. You've just got to look where no-one else is looking, and not be freaked by the dead woman.

Margot Excuse me?

Leyton Nothing. Just . . . you've gotta have money, that's what I'm saying. And if there *is* a dead woman involved, well in that kind of situation, in a dead-woman-between-you-and-a-pile-of-money situation, well you've got to go for the fuck-it-who-cares option. Haven't you?

Margot In as much as I understand a word your saying, no.

Leyton Oh. Well, we'll agree to differ then. Do you want to go out with me sometime?

Margot No.

Leyton Shit. How do you make eyes at a woman?

Margot Excuse me?

Leyton You know when people wink at each other and fucking smile and all that. Make eye contact. I need a whatsit, a technique.

Margot Have you considered chloroform?

Leyton What?

Margot Nothing.

Leyton Was that a joke? I've got to get wise to those bastards. Everybody jokes around here, it's a fucking nightmare. Everyone's whatsit, ironical.

Margot If you really want to impress another person, you've got to try and be yourself. Be honest. Be sincere. People appreciate sincerity, I find.

Leyton Yeah? Right. Be honest. Okay. (*Slight pause.*) Your tits are just how I like 'em.

Margot looks at him for a few seconds.

Margot Perhaps we've got our wires crossed. Mr Grayson. Do you think we have the kind of relationship, where if you were ever in any kind of trouble you could come and talk to me about it?

Leyton I do, Margot. A talking-about-stuff relationship, yeah.

Margot Well, I was just wondering . . . could we move that relationship onto a slightly more superficial plane?

Leyton Huh? Eh? You mean . . .? Sure. Sure.

Margot Thanks. It's just you give me the creeps.

Short silence.

Leyton Knock knock.

Margot What?

Leyton Nothing. So anyway I'm just out walking.

Margot Sure, you enjoy yourself, and others.

Leyton Just strolling up this way.

Margot Wouldn't go that way at this time. The red light district's just up there, unless you want to be accosted by prostitutes in stockings I'd take a right turn and walk down by the canal.

Leyton Ahhhhhh, no, I'm set on this way, I'll be okay.

Margot It's anything goes up there I'm telling you. Women offer bizarre sex services in exchange for money.

Leyton I'll take my chances. Thanks. I'm just walking.

He exits. Margot looks up at the sky and takes a deep breath.

Margot Can't stand here gazing up in awe all night, I've got work tomorrow. Pack it in you countless twinklers, there's people down here expecting post in the morning. . . . Just who exactly would turn their back on life, unless they hadn't looked up lately . . . shwwww . . .

She exits in the opposite direction to Leyton. Lights fade.

SCENE SEVEN

Vaughan's kitchen. Vaughan transferring ash from the packet into an urn. Hannah enters from upstairs.

Hannah Do you know where the key is to the spare room, Daddy? Oliver sleepwalks, apparently, through a shop window on one occasion.

Vaughan Princess, without being mean or anything, I'm not sure it's a good idea encouraging Oliver to stay here too long.

Hannah I feel sorry for him, don't you?

Vaughan Not wishing to sound macabre, but it might be better all round if he were dead and we were going through his pockets. I mean he'll attract attention, won't he, word will spread and people will say 'Let's all go and see the man who jumped from the bridge and survived.'

45

Hannah I feel as though he might be able to help us.

Vaughan I take the opposite view.

Hannah It's not a view, Daddy, it's a hunch.

Vaughan Hm?

Hannah It's an irrational inkling, an odd inner feeling, a hunch. I knew I'd have one one day.

Vaughan Well I don't like it, and neither would your mother have. We're cerebal people, I didn't read you the *Origin of Species* at bedtime for you to grow up to be a hunch-junkie.

Hannah His father was called The Terrier. That's the kind of nickname that inspires confidence.

Vaughan He's a loose cannon, and a ghost.

Hannah We could let him stay until he's well enough and then drop little hints.

Vaughan Or, coming at the issue from another angle, we could ask him to sling his hook in the morning, how about that?

Hannah We don't want to do that though, because we're not bad people.

Vaughan Well it wouldn't be hard-heartedness, Sweets, it'd be a love of your mother and a basic grasp of economics. It's a struggle to feed ourselves at the moment, let alone another mouth.

Hannah Let's see how it goes.

Vaughan If you-know-who comes by, well, he was very clear about not calling the police.

Hannah But Oliver's not a policeman.

Vaughan No but he does a good impression.

Hannah Maybe it's time we asked help of someone anyway.

Vaughan bangs his fist on the table.

Vaughan No, no, it's not time, no! (*stands*) I won't hear of it!

Short silence.

Hannah I'll prop a chair against the door if the key's not around.

Vaughan You changed the subject, Princess.

Hannah I know. Goodnight, Daddy.

Vaughan We weren't discussing the key or the door.

Hannah No. Goodnight, Daddy.

She kisses him on the cheek.

Vaughan Goodnight, Hannah.

Exit Hannah upstairs. Vaughan peers at the urn as the lights fade.

SCENE EIGHT

Reg's lounge. Reg at the door with Margot.

Margot Sorry I'm so late, I was too amazed to sleep again last night. (*Hands him some packets.*) I've got three here for you.

Reg Great, great, wow. I can't tell you how excited I am.

Margot Music, what a gift that is.

Reg It certainly is. 'Specially Denzil Golden.

Margot Wafting out of open windows – the first few bars of a favourite song, and it takes you back to some daft place you'd half forgotten. Big silly grin all over your face and everyone around you thinks you've lost your mind.

Reg I know what you mean, I really do.

Margot Magazine for Mr Grayson too.

She hands Reg a magazine.

Reg Oh, his *Motiveless Crimes* thing, thanks. Thanks . . .

Margot I don't know how he can read that stuff, but still.

Reg No I don't either . . . He's always had a streak of . . . and recently it's not even been a streak, it's been . . . way more than a streak . . . I tell you, Margot, I'm starting to worry about what's in that head of his.

Margot Funny peculiar you should say that, Reg. Some of my conversations with him have given me cause for concern lately, if you don't mind me being candid.

Reg No, God, of course I don't Margot. What kind of conversations?

Margot Well maybe I'm taking this out of context and there's some surreal humour behind this that I'm not aware of, but the other day he seemed to be preoccupied with a dead woman.

Reg A dead woman?

Margot Uh-huh. And he seemed to think that it was okay to use this . . . dead woman to make money.

Reg He . . . told you that?

Reg quietly puts the urn in a cupboard.

Margot Maybe I'm missing the point. But wouldn't you say that making money off of . . . maybe I'm old fashioned, but . . .

Reg No, no, it's wrong, isn't it, Margot? It's just plain wrong, even if you need the money, it's . . . disrespectful. And let me run this by you a second, just while we're throwing ideas around: would you say the idea of masturbating over the cremated remains of a stranger was perverse?

A moment's disbelief from Margot.

Margot Yes I would.

Reg Me too.

Margot Perverse is exactly the word I'd plump for there, Reg.

Reg You've got to have some kind of moral parameters, haven't you?

Margot Yes, you have.

Reg We're human beings, there's no reason to give in to every impulse is there, not when you can stop and think and . . . rationalise. I mean ever since Leyton lost his job it's like he's a different person, like a savage, I mean he's really taken the whole thing hard . . .

Margot I didn't realise he was so close to the edge. I really should've been more supportive, I was downright rude to him earlier.

Reg No, no, it's not your fault, Margot, I'm his older brother, I'm the one who needs to sort this all out with him, I've let this go way too far . . .

Margot Well, I'm going to be a bit more sensitive from now on, Reg. Give his confidence a bit of a boost, it sounds as though he needs it.

Reg Thanks Margot. Yes. And don't you worry, I'm going to have this out with him. Too far is too far, there's got to be a line. Thanks a lot.

Margot No problem. See you tomorrow.

Reg Yes, see you.

Margot starts to exit.

Margot . . . Something like 'California Dreaming', that sort of song . . . just comes on the radio and nearly lifts you out of your shoes . . .

She's gone. Reg closes door, opens first record and puts it on. Music. Reg goes to the cupboard, takes out the urn and looks at it.

Reg Too far is too far, Leyton.

Lights fade.

SCENE NINE

Vaughan's kitchen. Oliver and Hannah. Oliver looking out of window.

Oliver No, I'm sorry Hannah, I still don't see anything. All I see is a dirty old river and a factory that doesn't look as though it's made anything in a while. Give me a clue.

Hannah I was drawing your attention to The Morning You Almost Didn't See.

Oliver How d'you mean? Oh! Oh I get it, I'm with you, the morning in general, that's subtle, I wouldn't have got that in a million years. (*sighs*) I'm no Wolfgang Jensen, am I?

Hannah Who?

Oliver Highest I.Q. ever recorded, 197.

Hannah Oh. So I was drawing your attention to The Morning You Almost Didn't See to make you realise how incredible it is that you're standing here not appreciating my subtlety. Standing here instead of lying face down and bloated in that dirty river out there, I thought that might inspire you.

Oliver Inspire me? Wow. Inspire me . . . in what way exactly?

Hannah I prayed for someone to come, you see. Not to God, I couldn't face him, just to myself, just under my breath as I went to sleep.

Oliver Yes . . .?

Hannah And then there was you. Falling out of the sky, like an angel.

Oliver Or a suicidal salesman.

Hannah You might have been sent to help us. By Mummy.

Oliver Mummy who?

Hannah Mummy often got men to do things for her. The uniform. In a way it does fit you. In a way it's tailor-made.

Oliver Not unless the tailor was drunk, or, or aged about eight or something . . .

Hannah You're the son of The Terrier after all. That's a name that inspires confidence.

Oliver Oh yes, and he earned his reputation, Dad did. Didn't know the meaning of the word 'failure'. Did you ever hear of a man called The Beast UK?

Hannah I think so, on the radio once, just before Daddy rushed in and turned it off.

Oliver He went around chopping people up, what a loony. That's him.

He takes out the artist's impression from his father's notebook and shows it to Hannah.

Oliver His victims were all keen caravanners. It had a major impact on caravan sales for a while.

Hannah The Beast UK, that's not a reassuring nickname at all.

Oliver He used to just call himself The Beast, but he had to change when a sociopath in America threatened to sue for breach of copyright. Anyway, my dad looked after that case.

Hannah And brought his evil tyranny to an end, hurray.

Short silence.

Oliver No, that was the one case he never solved actually. It rankled with him too, that a homicidal maniac escaped justice like that. Never gave up trying to find him, though, he had the heart of a lion, Dad did. Uncle Victor was the same, he was a courageous man, a bodyguard in the United States for a while. Protected some of the biggest names you could think of – John F. Kennedy, Martin Luther King . . . John Lennon . . .

Hannah I'm sure if you tried you could be just like them. You could start today, in this very house.

Oliver No, I must've been adopted or switched with another baby at birth or something.

Hannah You could help us with all the trouble that we're having.

Oliver I'd be happy to help after all you've done for me. You know when I went outside to try and defumigate my shoes earlier, I noticed your gutters could do with clearing out, I'll do that if you want.

Hannah No, it doesn't matter about the gutters.

Oliver It'll matter in the long term, Hannah, clogged gutters are the catalyst to all sorts of later problems. A man selling gutter cleaning products let me in on that little secret.

Hannah The thing is, we're not as happy as we look in this house.

Oliver You aren't?

Hannah No. Actually sometimes I'll be doing something and I'll find I'm on the brink of tears even though I haven't been peeling onions or stubbed my toe. And you wouldn't expect to be on the brink of tears just like that would you?

Oliver Speaking just as a lay-person now, I'd say no – but I'm not an expert, never have been.

Hannah Sometimes Daddy lets out a baleful moan and suddenly breaks plates.

Oliver Again, I'd say that's a sign there's something wrong, you should tell this to someone.

Hannah I am. To you.

Oliver No, I mean someone who isn't a congenital dunderhead.

Hannah I'm shy.

Oliver But you're telling me, and we've only just met.

Hannah I'm having an unguarded moment. You see although I love Daddy, he –

Enter Vaughan, dragging a dead swan.

Vaughan Now then.

Hannah Poor swan.

Vaughan Poor heavy swan. (*Rubs his back.*) Fat bloody swan.

53

Oliver Did you kill this?

Vaughan No, it was under the bridge. It happens now and then. We find all sorts. There was a pair of cows under there not long ago which, you know, is a mad event.

Hannah Perhaps they all jumped.

Vaughan Perhaps, though I can't help thinking you're anthropomorphising a little bit, Hannah. We'll need to pluck it, won't we, and would we need to deal with giblets?

Oliver I don't want to speak out of turn, but have you considered the possibility that these birds might be mildly or totally poisonous?

Vaughan I think you are mistaken.

Hannah But you don't know either Daddy.

Vaughan No, Flower, but I think he's mistaken.

Hannah *Think* though, Daddy, that's all.

Vaughan is surprised by Hannah taking Oliver's side, and looks at her in a puzzled manner. Short silence.

Vaughan We'll cook it and eat it carefully then. Boil it, that'll clean its tubes out nicely.

Hannah Alright, that should do it, yes. (*to Oliver*) Are you hungry?

Oliver Oh, haven't you done enough for me already . . .?

Vaughan (*offering hand*) Good point, keep in touch won't you?

Hannah We'd like you to stay. Love you to. Please. Otherwise you'll come across as rude.

Vaughan hands Oliver his coat.

Vaughan At the same time, though, we don't want to keep you from anything and there's nothing worse than a welcome out-stayed.

Oliver Of course. I'll go.

Oliver takes his coat. Hannah blocks the door.

Hannah You. Will come across. As rude.

Oliver I wouldn't want to seem rude after all you've done for me, of course not.

Hannah It's agreed then, good. I'll set the table.

Hannah goes and gets knives and forks and starts to set the table. Oliver puts his coat down.

Vaughan (*sighs*) . . . Yes . . . great then . . . stay for dinner then . . . that's the best idea, you hang around a while . . . and be spooky . . . yes . . . why not . . . great news . . .

A knock at the door.

Vaughan Door? It can't be, Hannah you don't think it's – ?

Hannah Look through the letter-box.

Vaughan Right. Calmly look through the letter-box.

Vaughan goes to letter-box and looks through.

It's the Postmanwoman. We're okay, it's the Postman-woman.

He opens the door. It is indeed Margot.

Margot Howdy.

Vaughan Crikey yes, howdy's right and anyone who says we've got a crisis on our hands is a liar.

Margot (*points outside*) There was a bird on your tree just then, I took a quick photo of it but then I had to get on due to my workload.

Vaughan Shame.

Margot Here you go. Package for . . . your wife.

She hands him a small package.

Vaughan Oh. Oh.

Margot Hope I'm not raking up painful memories.

Vaughan Er . . . no . . . no . . . something for my darling dead wife . . . good . . .

Margot It's always hard to forget someone you've loved. Me, I start by forgetting the feet then work my way up. I can't remember my mother's legs any more, and her waist is slightly blurry, which is not bad after only six years. Another decade or so and I'll have no recollection of her long red hair and her eye-patch. All that'll be left will be a tap-tap-tap sound.

Vaughan Tap-tap-tap, yes. Death's mocking finger on the window-pane.

Margot No, typewriter keys. She started writing a novel about the eternal triangle but she never worked out how to end it.

Vaughan begins unwrapping the packet. Margot notices Oliver for the first time.

Margot Oh. Excuse me. A policeman, huh? Is everything alright?

Oliver Oh I'm not really –

Vaughan He'll be going soon, without incident.

Hannah He jumped from the bridge.

Margot He never did.

56

Hannah It's true. He jumped from the very top and hasn't got a scratch. This is the man you saw jump yesterday.

Margot That's quite a feat. Nobody's ever done that before.

Hannah I think he's special.

Oliver Oh I think special's a bit strong, it was nothing really.

Margot I'd say special. A two hundred and twelve foot drop into rocky water with a notorious current, that takes some surviving.

Oliver Well . . . I suppose it does, doesn't it . . .

Margot You're a real-life human interest story. How'd you do it?

Oliver Twh, I don't know, I think I probably managed to relax my body, by just, you know, fainting.

Vaughan (*showing everyone*) It's a cigarette lighter.

Margot (*to Oliver*) Would you mind if I took your photo?

Oliver Say again?

Margot This is exactly the kind of thing I've been waiting for, you see I've just written this pamphlet about the bridge that you jumped from – take one, they're free –

She hands Oliver a pamphlet.

Oliver – Oh, thanks . . .

Vaughan . . . See? (*He flicks it on.*) She collected tokens for months for this . . .

Margot – I've been trying to counter its unfortunate reputation, and I really think your story could be useful, if you don't mind?

Oliver Not at all, of course not . . .

Margot takes out an instant camera and Oliver poses cheesily.

Margot It was William Corp's favourite piece of work, he called it 'the triumph of creativity over practicality'.

Oliver . . . Do you want me over here, by the window, I could point out at the bridge . . .?

Margot That'd be great, fantastic . . .

Vaughan . . . She had to smoke her way through hundreds of cigarettes to get this, but when she put her mind to something there was no stopping the woman . . .

Margot takes a couple of photos as Oliver adopts some poses.

Margot (*taking photos*) . . . It makes a change to have a happy story associated with it . . . this could really turn things around . . . you know, The Bridge Of Miracles, that kind of angle . . .

Oliver Do you think so?

Vaughan . . . She'd smoke all night and all day, you've got to admire that . . .

Margot The media love zany stories with an upbeat slant. Hey, you know the camera really loves you, you're a natural at this . . .

Oliver A natural, eh? Thanks.

Margot (*stops photographing*) It's been a pleasure to meet you.

She shakes hands with him.

Good luck with the future.

Oliver Thanks.

Margot Futures are lovely. You all take care now.

Hannah Goodbye.

Vaughan Yes . . . she got there in the end . . .

Margot exits and Hannah closes the door after her.

Hannah I love our postmanwoman, don't you?

Oliver Who'd've thought it, me of use to someone?

Hannah You could be of use to lots of people.

Vaughan *It isn't fair, of course. It isn't fair, but what's the use crying about it.*

Short silence.

Hannah (*to Oliver*) If you want to make an excuse to leave us alone, don't let me stop you.

Oliver Oh! Right . . . er . . . I'm just going to . . . freshen up . . . er . . .

Exit Oliver. Hannah puts her arm around Vaughan.

Hannah It's going to be alright, Daddy. Oliver will help us.

Vaughan What?

Hannah I prayed, Daddy. Under my breath as I went to sleep, and then, out of the blue –

Vaughan He's got to go.

Hannah No he hasn't, Daddy.

Vaughan He's got to go, otherwise we're practically arguing.

Hannah He can help us.

Vaughan He'll ruin everything. Ruin it to bits.

Hannah He's special.

Vaughan He's an odd-ball and we haven't been this close to arguing since that time you decided to henna your hair.

Hannah We need to learn to trust someone, someone good, and special, who's got what it takes to be a hero. The son of The Terrier.

Short silence.

Vaughan How can you think, Princess, that that man is . . . special?

Short silence.

Hannah Not think, Daddy. *Feel.*

Oliver re-enters with the handle from the toilet.

Oliver I, er, I broke your toilet.

Hannah Oh.

Short silence.

Oliver But I'm going to fix it. Don't you worry. Really.

Oliver begins to back out nervously. Vaughan picks up the swan and slams it into the sink.

Oliver (*exiting*) I'll make everything fine.

He's gone. Short silence.

Hannah He will, Daddy. I know he will.

The lights fade. Music.

Interval

Act Two

Reg's lounge. Reg is tied to a chair. Leyton stands over him with a cigarette in one hand and a hammer in the other. Several broken records lie in pieces on the table.

Leyton Okay, what's next? What we got left here . . .

Takes a last puff on his cigarette, then drops it. Picks up a record, takes it out of its sleeve and reads the label.

Chemical Toilet, Volume One.

Reg Oh God, not the Chemical Toilet, Leyton. That's rare.

Leyton The urn, Reg.

Reg That's just literally irreplaceable.

Leyton Where's the fucking urn?

Reg grits his teeth and starts to sob softly. Leyton sighs, casually breaks the record with the hammer and picks up another. Reads the label.

Chemical Toilet, Volume Two.

Reg I've wet myself.

Leyton Guest starring Prince Sammy 'Pops' Montana Junior.

Reg I have actually physically wet myself.

Leyton (*squinting at sleeve notes*) 'A shifting cathedral of eclectic electric kaleidoscopic mood-fish a-leaping through waves of blues-funk-Afro-retro-fusion.' Huh? A shifting cathedral . . . of eclectic electric . . .

Breaks record casually.

Leyton That's gotta fucking go. Some of those words were three inches long.

Reg Leyton – I'm saving you from yourself, I can see where you're going to end up at this rate and it's not a nice place. Everyone knows there's got to be a line, and that too far is too far, and that's exactly how far you've gone, too far.

Leyton Where'd you hide the urn, Reg?

Reg Let's debate the issues. Let's have a frank exchange of opinions, but leave the Denzil Golden stuff, huh?

Leyton Where is it?

Reg Please, I'm fraught here, you only have to look at the state of my trousers to see how fraught I am.

Leyton picks up another record. Reads cover.

Leyton 'Diabolical Chariots.'

Reg Not that! For God's sake, that's a one off!

Leyton (*takes out sleeve and reads lyrics*) 'A Rover's Blues . . . Man I wanted to be a farmer / But I didn't have the chicken-craft, no / Said I wanted to be a farmer . . . ' What the hell is this about? Chicken-craft, what the fuck's chicken-craft? . . .

Reg Alright Leyton, I'll tell you where the urn is, I've cracked here now. I give in.

Leyton I'm glad about that Reg. I hate to see you like this. It's undignified.

Reg Boy oh boy, I tell you, you need a resolve of iron or underpants of rubber . . .

Leyton Where's the urn?

Reg Second cupboard down on the left.

Leyton retrieves the urn from the cupboard.

Let me go now, Leyton. I'm disappointed in myself and I've gotta get out of these trousers.

Leyton Na-ah. I'd like to, but the fact of the matter is you're a treacherous bastard Reg. I can't take the chance of letting you go.

Reg I think you can, I really do.

Leyton opens the urn. Takes out a small packet of ash from inside it.

Leyton (*starts to leave*) I'm with-holding your share of the money today, Reg. You don't deserve it. You've cost me half an afternoon.

Reg I'm seeing a whole different side to your personality recently. Let me go would you?

Leyton No can do. You can stay here with your poverty and your cathedrals of eclectic chickens. Me, I've got The Pleasure-Grapple wrestling club to finance.

He exits and closes door behind him.

Reg Come on now, Leyton. Let me go. Leyton? Leyton!

Lights fade.

SCENE ELEVEN

Vaughan's kitchen. Vaughan, Hannah and Oliver eating the swan. Vaughan is picking at his food. Oliver has lots of his food on his jacket.

Hannah Aren't you hungry, Daddy?

Vaughan Ravenous. But I can't work out how to eat and worry at the same time.

Hannah You seem to be enjoying it Oliver?

Oliver It's a bit like duck, isn't it, a bigger version of the more traditional dish of duck . . .

Hannah Do you think so?

Oliver Yes, don't you?

Hannah I don't remember. It's a long while since we had duck. We had baked otter not that long ago.

Vaughan It's funny, my mouth's watering at the smell and yet my stomach's in knots like you wouldn't believe. And even though I've been to the toilet three times, I've got a strong urge to go again.

Oliver I'm a member of the Spastic Colon club too, Vaughan.

Vaughan No it's not a colonic problem. I think it's more along the lines of Dread.

Oliver Dread? Oh.

Vaughan A terrible sense of lives unravelling.

Oliver Oh. Well, that wouldn't be any of my business then.

Vaughan No, it wouldn't. Why not try eating really quickly, just for a bit of fun?

Hannah Daddy. I've been thinking.

Vaughan Enough pillows for you last night, Oliver?

Oliver Oh yes thank you Vaughan. Slept like a log, and no Rat Tat Ginger dreams either.

Hannah You changed the subject Daddy.

Vaughan Like a log, eh? A strange human log, I'm so glad.

Hannah We weren't discussing pillows.

Oliver I might leave this last piece if you don't mind, I tend to overdo it. I've even thrown up through over-eating before now. But that was lovely. Well I probably ought to be going.

Vaughan (*standing*) Maybe you ought to quickly run out the back way just to see what it feels like.

Hannah No. That's what I was trying to say, Daddy, Oliver has to stay.

Vaughan Maybe with your overcoat buttoned right up, totally covering your uniform. Not for any reason at all, just to pass the time of day.

A knock at the door.

Too late. Too late, now look. I told you. Gigantic trouble now.

Hannah We shouldn't panic. We should be calm or even light-hearted.

Oliver Well I ought to be making tracks, but I want to thank you –

Vaughan Out the back way, quick!

Oliver (*grabbing coat*) Right you are.

Hannah No!

Vaughan Hannah don't take this the wrong way, but are you losing your lovely marbles?

Hannah No, you've got to stay.

Another, louder knock. Hannah forces Oliver back down into the sitting position.

Vaughan Hannah, this is – Where's the tooth? Where's the jar – Ah!

Vaughan grabs the jar, and takes out the gold tooth and five pound note. Scurries towards the door, pausing briefly by Oliver.

Vaughan (*to Oliver*) Still here?

Vaughan then rushes to the door and opens it very quickly.

Leyton 'Bout fucking time, I –

By this time Vaughan has closed the door behind him so that he and Leyton are both outside. We can only hear muffled snatches of their conversation.

Oliver The trouble that you mentioned, Hannah.

Hannah Yes?

Oliver Is this anything to do with it?

Hannah Yes.

Leyton (*off*) A gold fucking *tooth*?

More animated conversation behind the door. The door bursts open, then is suddenly slammed shut again. It should be evident that Vaughan is trying to stop Leyton getting into the house.

(*off*) Out of the way, old timer!

Hannah It sounds like Daddy is being duffed up.

Oliver Do you think that's what that sound is? I was wondering.

Hannah I'm sure you've got a plan though. You must have, being our only hope.

Oliver Oh. (*Clears throat.*) When you say 'Your only hope' . . .

Leyton bursts in, followed by Vaughan crawling on his knees and nursing a bloody nose. Hannah stands but Oliver remains where he is. Leyton stares at Oliver a while, then looks at Hannah, then at Vaughan, then points to Oliver.

Leyton I didn't fucking touch him. (*Points to Vaughan.*) He fell. Here, look, I'm helping him up.

Helps Vaughan to his feet.

Vaughan He didn't punch me anywhere, let alone in the face.

Leyton There's no way there's any crime in that, he just fucking fell.

Vaughan I just fell. Down.

Hannah This is Oliver Hoff. He's a policeman.

Oliver Oh not really, Hannah, I mean –

Hannah They call him The Terrier because he always gets his man.

Oliver Actually that was my Dad . . .

Leyton There's no fucking man to get here, I don't know what she's told you but this is a fucking false alarm.

Vaughan Here here.

Hannah He's really ruthless and he especially doesn't like sneaky extorters, do you?

Oliver Well, no . . . of course not, but . . .

Leyton This guy just fell. She's bananas, she's a woman. They confide in cats for Christ's sake. They'll fucking mutter away to cats for hours, women will, tell them their secrets, they're all nuts. (*to Vaughan*) I said no police.

Vaughan We can explain.

Leyton I fucking trusted you and now there's this police-involved situation.

Vaughan We can explain at length –

Leyton (*to Oliver*) I'm not a criminal.

Oliver Well that's great, sir, because I'm not a policeman, so that's great.

Leyton Shit, that's irony isn't it.

Oliver No.

Leyton Everyone around here's ironical in tone.

Hannah (*to Leyton*) He's quite prepared to bend the rules if he thinks it's justified.

Oliver Look, okay, okay, let's all just try and calm down. I wouldn't want things to turn nasty.

Leyton Are you threatening me?

Oliver No, no, I'm just saying take it easy.

Vaughan – It's not as it seems, you'll laugh when you –

Leyton I'm going to report you to the police complaints place.

Oliver But I'm not a policeman.

Leyton You've got codes of conduct and shit to stick to.

Hannah No he hasn't.

Leyton Yes he has! I wanna talk to a lawyer!

Oliver Oh come on, we don't need lawyers, we can straighten this out here and now, just the two of us.

Oliver moves towards Leyton with his arms out in friendliness, but Leyton picks up a chair to fend him off.

Leyton No way, you can't do this, you can't lay a finger on me, that'd be un-policemany fucking behaviour, or, or –

Oliver Let me take my jacket off –

Oliver begins to take his jacket off.

Leyton You keep away from me! I'm not fighting you! You can't do this! I've done nothing, get this guy away from me!

Leyton drops the chair and exits, running for his life.

Vaughan Wait!

Oliver I'm sorry, I thought if I took the uniform off –

Hannah You scared him off!

Oliver Do you think so? Pwh, I've never scared anyone before in my life – except a whole bunch of driving instructors.

Hannah Are you alright, Daddy?

Vaughan Do you know, I really don't know how to answer that question any more, Princess.

Hannah It'll be better now, Daddy, now that we've unveiled our secret weapon.

She looks admiringly at Oliver.

Oliver Who, me?

Vaughan (*to Oliver*) Still here then?

Hannah (*also to Oliver*) You're a mystic saviour.

Vaughan I might go and lie down.

Hannah Good idea, Daddy.

Vaughan Draw the curtains and lie staring at the ceiling for a few days.

Hannah A lie-down's just what's called for.

Vaughan (*going*) . . . I'm just off to turn things over and over in my mind for ages . . .

Exit Vaughan. Short silence.

Hannah So, what's the plan?

Oliver Plan? Plan . . .

Hannah The brilliant foolproof plan, yes. You can tell me.

Oliver I'm not so sure I can, you know . . .

Hannah Maybe you'd like to know everything that's happened? Mummy died, that's when it started. And Daddy had her remains put in an urn . . .

Lights begin slowly fading.

Oliver . . . I'm not a very good listener, actually . . .

Hannah He used to take her everywhere, and one day he took her with him to the park . . .

Oliver . . . Maybe you'd like to hear some interesting world records . . .

Blackness now.

SCENE TWELVE

The bridge. Margot is sticking photos of Oliver every-where. Leyton enters.

Margot Howdy Mr Gray – Leyton. I was hoping I'd see you. Have you got a minute?

Leyton Hm? Oh. Hi. Fuck. It's not a good time, I'm in a – Okay, what? What d'you want?

Margot I just wanted to apologise for earlier. Calling you a creep.

Leyton pulls off one of the photos of Oliver and stares at it.

(*after a second or two*) Mr – Leyton? (*Beat.*) Nice photo, huh?

Leyton What the – ? Who the – ?

Margot The camera really loves him, doesn't it? Did you hear what he did? Jumped off this bridge and got away without a scratch.

Leyton He fucking *what*?

She begins blowing up a balloon. In between puffs she speaks.

Margot It's a miracle don't you think? I guess The Man Upstairs looked on him kindly due to his good work. Policemen are generally on the side of the good guys, aren't they, do a good service despite constant allegations of corruption.

Leyton This guy, he jumped and – ?

Margot nods. She ties off the balloon and turns it into an animal.

Margot I watched him do it – boy I've got to stop smoking, my lungs are packing in on me.

Leyton Jesus. He's fucking indestructible. He's some sort of superman.

Margot It's the kind of story that can change a bridge's reputation. I've already got two TV stations interested, they're on the way down here even as we speak. (*deep breath*) Just can't resist those Cuban cigars, well you've got to treat yourself sometimes, haven't you?

Leyton Fuck. He's just lucky though right? As opposed to, whatsit, supernatural?

Margot Well it makes you wonder, doesn't it? It's nice to think there might be a Grand Conductor up there running things, making sure dogs bark at thunder and mothers cry at weddings.

Leyton You think he's some kind of avenging angel guy?

Margot (*shows animal*) Giraffe, what d'you think? . . . Avenging, avenging what?

Leyton Nothing. There's no avenging needed . . . Shit no . . . What do you think the dead do?

Margot Begging your pardon?

Leyton You think they just lie there and rot, or . . . I mean they just lie there and rot, right? Or if they're burnt they just . . . Once they're burnt they're burnt, right? They don't . . . come back?

Margot Who knows? Me, I'm just grateful for this world and if there's another on the other side, well that's a bonus.

Leyton One dead woman couldn't call a dead policeman though, that'd be a crazy kind of heaven . . .

Margot Best not to monkey around with the dead too much, just in case. (*Blows balloon.*) Fancy blowing up a few of these? (*Offers balloons.*) The sausagey ones are going to give me a stroke.

Leyton No, I gotta go. I'm freaked now, I gotta get back.

Margot Well listen, Leyton, this avenging angel idea of yours is the kind of thing TV people love. Why don't you hang around and tell them all about it?

Leyton I gotta go. I gotta fucking, I'm, Jesus, I'm –

He's off, sharpish.

Margot (*as he goes*) We could maybe go for a drink after or something . . .? Hm. Must be losing my touch.

Music. Lights fade, as she tapes another balloon animal on the bridge.

SCENE THIRTEEN

Vaughan's kitchen. Music fades. Hannah and Oliver are walking backwards in circles, with Hannah resting one hand on Oliver's shoulder and feeling for obstacles with the other.

Hannah It's not nearly as . . . easy as you'd – ow! – think, is it? . . .

Oliver Imagine doing this . . . all the way from – whoops! – Santa Monica to . . . Istanbul . . .

Hannah That's a long way when you're . . . deliberately walking backwards.

Oliver Over eight thousand miles in total. You'd think he'd be a household name.

Hannah What was his name?

Oliver Plennie L. Wingo, of Abilene, Texas.

Hannah I expect before he did that everybody thought that Plennie was just an ordinary man . . . Ow! . . . Can we stop now, please, I'm going a bit mad?

Oliver Me too.

They stop, and Oliver rocks dizzily for a second before grabbing Hannah for support and then slumping into

a chair. Short silence, then Hannah picks up the
photograph of her mother and gazes at it.

Hannah Tell me another bizarre or amazing world record.

Oliver Really? No-one's ever been interested in my knowledge of records before, this is great, let me think now . . . Oh! Try believing this one then: the longest recorded ride in full armour is 167 miles, set by Dick Brown in 1979.

Hannah I expect before he rode all that way in armour everyone thought Dick Brown was a little boring.

Oliver Well, if they did he made them eat their words.

Hannah Yes. He revealed his hidden talents.

She places the photo of her mother down directly in front of Oliver.

Oliver . . . Yes . . . and the largest ever . . . beard of bees was . . . You're still thinking about your mother, aren't you, Hannah? I can tell.

Hannah You've seen through me, I *am* still thinking about her, even though the beard of bees sounded intriguing, I can't help it. But I'm not worried at all because you're here now.

Oliver Uh-huh . . . I'm an unlikely looking hero though, aren't I?

Hannah You're bound to be, it's an unlikely problem.

Oliver I hadn't thought of that.

Hannah And who's to say Plennie Wingo and Dick Brown didn't look unlikely too? Before they walked backwards or rode in full armour? But they managed to change themselves, like caterpillars change into butterflies.

Oliver . . . Yes, they do do that, don't they, and no-one thinks that's odd . . .

Hannah Or like tadpoles change into frogs.

Oliver . . . Yeah . . . or like . . . like crocodiles change into handbags.

Hannah . . . Hmmm . . . less so, but why not.

Oliver I guess everybody laughed at Dick and Plennie too, that's why they did it, to prove a point.

Hannah No-one's laughing now they're in the book of world records.

Oliver No . . . and no-one was laughing when I stepped up that time to get the award for colouring-in . . . Well, a few were, but only the Sports teachers . . .

Hannah You were a hero then. Remember, you're the son of The Terrier, after all, who never failed to solve a single case.

Oliver Yes. Except The Beast UK one.

Hannah You should never forget that you're a man who looked death full in the face.

Oliver I did, yes . . . I had forgotten that.

Hannah That shows you're a man of courage.

Oliver takes out a pen and writes something on the back of his hand.

Oliver (*writing*) . . . Courage, yes, must remember that. I'm a man of courage.

Hannah And spontaneity.

Oliver Right.

He writes this down on his hand again.

Oliver I'm a man of courage and spontaneity.

Hannah And honesty.

Oliver tries to add 'honesty' to his hand but there's no room.

Oliver I haven't got room for honesty, I'll just have to remember that one.

Hannah Okay. Courage and spontaneity are the main two anyway.

She takes the pen off him and writes on the back of her hand.

I'll take honesty, shall I, it's a shame to see it go to waste.

Oliver Oliver Hoff. Ex-lacklustre salesman but now transformed into a man of (*reads*) courage and spontaneity.

Hannah Hurray.

Oliver So . . . that character earlier, the man who has your mother . . . Do you know him?

Hannah Only well enough to really not like him. I bet he deliberately steps on snails, only joking.

Oliver Because one of the interesting things I learnt from Dad is that most victims of crime know their assailants. He said it would reduce the figures hugely if people made a greater effort not to meet.

Hannah I know he lives in Diesel Terrace, on the other side of the bridge. I followed him once, hoping my rage would suddenly erupt from my bestial soul leading me to bash him on the head with something blunt, like a box. But it didn't, of course.

Oliver What number Diesel Terrace would that be?

Hannah Number nought.

Oliver Number nought? That's probably number ten – the numbers fall off sometimes, you've got to watch for that, it's confusing.

Hannah (*delighted*) Now you've said something clever.

Oliver Thanks . . . so number ten Diesel Terrace, over the bridge . . . and, do you think he's dangerous?

Hannah Oh I expect so. He punched Daddy. I don't believe Daddy fell over at all.

Oliver Neither do I, what a pair of cynics.

Hannah The thing is, we've got less than half of Mummy back, and now he knows you're on the trail he might be tempted to do something dastard-minded with the rest of her.

Oliver Good point, yes.

Hannah I suppose what I'm saying is, it's urgent.

Oliver Right, right. Urgent and dangerous are the two key words then, good.

Hannah I bet in a second or two you're going to spring into action.

Oliver Yeeeees . . . 'course I am . . .

Very, very slowly Oliver begins to get up, focusing all the time on his hand.

Hannah I knew it! I knew it! You're springing!

Oliver Here he goes then, the all-new Oliver Hoff!

In slow motion he gets to his feet and begins to head for the door.

Hannah You're rescuing Mummy, albeit slowly!

Oliver . . . Number ten . . . Diesel Terrace . . .

Hannah Just over the bridge and down to your right!

Hannah is bouncing on her toes with excitement. Oliver moves very slowly towards the door.

Oliver His legs don't want to move but he won't let that stop him.

Hannah Hurray, although it seems painstaking!

Hannah opens door for him.

Oliver The all new jelly-kneed hero departs . . .

Hannah Hurray!

Oliver . . . Olly Hoff is on the case . . . ignoring the voice in his head that's screaming 'Sit back down you chubby loon' . . .

Hannah Good luck! Good luck!

Oliver has finally made it out of the door, still staring at his hand. Hannah closes the door. Lights fade.

SCENE FOURTEEN

Reg's lounge. Reg is trying to move himself out of the lounge, but every inch is a struggle. Leyton enters, flustered.

Leyton Reg! Reg! – How the fuck d'you manage to get over there?

Reg Well it wasn't easy Leyton, and I might've put my back out, I really think I've done myself a damage.

Leyton Yeah, well I've got other shit to worry about.

Reg You're really showing your true colours lately.

Leyton Shut up, I'm thinking.

Reg What's happened Leyton? You look pale as anything.

Leyton They got the police in.

Reg Ohhhhh lordy, Leyton, you've done it now. Now you've done it.

Leyton They said no police, I fucking trusted them and now look. Now what do I do? Huh?

Reg Well, there's nothing you can do, Leyton, you just got to throw yourself on their mercy.

Leyton Fuck no, he'll arrest me.

Reg Oh God, Leyton, I warned you about this, I said . . .

Leyton Shut up would you?

Reg We're in more trouble here than you could shake a stick at.

Leyton starts pouring himself a drink.

Leyton Bit of fucking whatsit, lateral thinking, that's what we've gotta do. Start laterally thinking Reg, quick as you can.

Reg God no, it's over Leyton, we've got to give ourselves up, this thing's out of control.

Leyton You wanna spend the next five years in gaol?

Reg They won't give us five years, it was only theft, like you said.

Leyton What? Shit, I get it. I get it, you treacherous little fucker. You're going to blame me. It's going to be, 'Hey I just found the urn, it was him who did the rest, send him to gaol, let *his* fucking ears grow down to his elbows in a fucking cell.' Well, no way, Reg. I'm going to get rid of the evidence. It's our word against theirs, he can't fucking touch us if he hasn't got proof.

Reg I'm turning myself in, and you should too.

Leyton I've seen the guy. He's the kind of guy who doesn't follow the rules, he does things his way, and the camera loves him. We don't get rid of that urn, we're sitting ducks.

Leyton picks up urn.

Reg Leyton, hey, untie me.

Leyton I'm doing this for both of us, Reg. But you breathe a word to this guy and I'm going to have to cut your fucking heart out and eat it, understand?

Reg That's a hell of an image to throw out at this point, but listen to me would you?

Leyton puts on shades, covers his face with a scarf.

Listen up, God almighty we're in real trouble, I beg you . . .

Leyton exits with the urn.

This isn't very brotherly of you, you know, Leyton!

Lights fade.

SCENE FIFTEEN

Vaughan's kitchen. Hannah is wrapping left-over swan in silver foil for sandwiches. Vaughan comes down from upstairs.

Hannah Are you feeling any better?

Vaughan I'm not really feeling anything, Sweets. I'm a man without a within at the moment.

Hannah Would a glass of water help?

Vaughan I think it would be neither here nor there, thank you. Where's Oliver Hoff?

Hannah He's gone.

Vaughan Phew. I have to say I'm glad, but the damage may be done.

Hannah No, he's gone to get Mummy.

Vaughan What?

Hannah He's sprung into action.

Vaughan You let him?

Hannah Um, well I didn't so much *let* him as . . . encourage him.

Vaughan You *encouraged* him? That's even worse, that's twice as bad again as even letting him, you must have toys in your head or something.

Hannah I haven't got toys in my head.

Vaughan Well you just must have, I'd've thought, the way you carry on, you must have all sorts of toys in your head.

Hannah That's horrible.

Vaughan You must be under his wily charming spell or something.

Hannah Well, you must just be jealous then.

Vaughan Jealous? In what way jealous?

Hannah I don't know, I just blurted it.

Vaughan Jealous how so? What are you trying to mean?

Hannah I don't know, that's why you shouldn't blurt, in case you blurt some old nonsense.

Vaughan Oh. Hm. Well if you –

Hannah Of him and me.

Vaughan What?

Hannah Maybe falling in love and leaving you here alone without me or Mummy, as a grief-stricken recluse.

Short silence.

Vaughan What?

Hannah Blurt, blurt, blurt that's all.

Vaughan You and him? Hannah? You and impossibly him?

Hannah Hold on, I just need a minute for this sick feeling to – (*She swallows, pats her chest, takes a breath.*) – that's better, I'm better now.

Vaughan Him and you? Fancy man and fancy woman? And me nothing but a grief-stricken recluse . . .?

Hannah You shouldn't blurt, that's all. But you said I had toys in my head and I got upset, and, and I didn't mean the grief-stricken recluse bit.

Silence. Vaughan just stares at his shoes.

Vaughan Of course I took your mother's death hard, I loved her, it's only natural.

Hannah I know.

Vaughan It's a quaint English tradition to be upset when your wife dies.

Hannah I know it is. I'm sorry, Daddy. I take everything back.

Vaughan (*sighs*) Alright, Princess. We're both a little tense. Let's forget this ever happened.

Hannah looks at what's written on the back of her hand.

Hannah Let's not.

Vaughan What?

Hannah I'm not sorry. And if we get Mummy back will it be better or worse, that's what I wonder.

Vaughan What? Better. Lots better, lots.

Hannah I've decided to think it might not be.

Vaughan Why?

Hannah Because it's not very normal to act as though she's still here even when she isn't. To take her everywhere with you, and talk to her, and ask her things when she isn't here to answer. Also, while I think of it, she wasn't nearly as nice as you make out, she drank and she swore and she threw things and she slept with all sorts of strange men.

Vaughan You – you – I –

Hannah She treated you so badly I'm not even sure she liked you.

Vaughan Your mother was – this is –

Hannah I half think she hated you.

Vaughan I hope you get thrown in an owl chamber!

Hannah screams in terror for a second, then recovers.

Hannah There's no such thing you batty shambles.

Vaughan I hope they throw you in a prototype then!

Hannah Now *you're* just blurting, you silly . . . thin . . . wreck.

Vaughan I know! (*Silence.*) I know . . .

Hannah She *died*, Daddy. She's gone. (*Pause.*) I'm sorry, I'm so – (*She looks at her hand and swallows hard.*) This is love too, Daddy. Saying this to you.

Vaughan Even as directly as that?

Hannah Yes. Yes, it's just a funny way of showing it.

Vaughan This is hardly music to my ears, Petal . . .

Hannah It has to be honest, Daddy. And I don't know if this is courage or just fatigue and maybe they're two different types of honesty and the one that comes from fatigue is harsher . . .

Vaughan . . . Quick sit down for me I think . . .

Slowly lowers himself onto the seat.

Hannah I'm sorry, Daddy.

Vaughan No, it's alright. It's just you threw me off a cliff there, not a real one of course.

Hannah Glass of water?

Vaughan Absolutely.

Hannah pours a glass of water and hands it to him.

Hannah You'll be alright, Daddy, in time.

Vaughan Yes . . . I expect so . . . I'm well-read, after all . . .

Hannah We'll both be fine. And I don't want to sound like a greetings card, but I'd do anything for you.

Hannah turns back to the window and notices something.

Daddy. Oh no. Daddy! He's up there on the bridge.

Vaughan turns to look. Lights fade.

The bridge. Margot and Leyton.

Margot Look, I know what this is about, Leyton. I spoke to Reg earlier.

Leyton What? That stupid – He *told* you?

Margot Yes. About how depressed you've been since losing your job. But do you really think jumping off here's going to solve anything?

Leyton What? I'm not jumping off here. What d'you think I am, fucking nuts?

Margot What are you doing here then?

Leyton Nothing. Jesus. I just wanna be alone for a minute, is that a fucking problem?

Margot 'Course not. You don't fancy . . . maybe going for a drink or something later?

Leyton Some other time.

Margot A walk then?

Leyton Nah.

Margot The TV people'll be here in a minute, it'll be quite exciting if you want to hang around?

Leyton No. N – O, Jesus woman, can't you take a hint? Leave me alone, would you?

Margot I didn't mean to interfere. It's just you seem a bit jumpy. (*winces*) Sorry, bad choice of word.

Leyton I'm not jumpy, who you calling fucking jumpy? I just want a couple of minutes alone.

Margot Right. I'll leave you be, then. I need to photo-copy some new pamphlets, so I'll just . . . (*Starts to go, stops.*) D'you want my phone number?

Leyton Just go! Jesus.

Margot Right. Okay. You take care now.

Margot exits. Leyton takes out the urn (from under his coat) and looks at it for a moment. Then he looks left and right anxiously, and finally holds the urn over the railings, ready to drop it.

Leyton No fucking evidence.

Blackout.

SCENE SEVENTEEN

Vaughan's kitchen. Vaughan and Hannah looking out of the window. They both gasp. Short silence.

Vaughan He's done it. He's dropped her. That's it then.

Lights fade.

SCENE EIGHTEEN

Reg's lounge. Reg, still tied to the chair, is desperately trying to move towards the door. After a moment or two of trying, there is a knock at the door. Reg hangs his head in despair.

Reg Our father who art in heaven, hallowed be thy name . . .

Very, very slowly the door opens and Oliver pokes just his head in.

Oliver I can come back. I'll come back.

He closes the door again. After a second or two he bursts back in, staring at the writing on the back of his hand.

Where's the urn, scumbag?

Reg I haven't got it! I haven't got it, I swear, my brother's got it!

Oliver Your brother? Is he a man about so high (*demonstrates*) with a mouth like a sewer?

Reg Yes, yes, that's him. You probably passed him, but he had on his hat and his sun-glasses. He said he was going to get rid of the evidence.

Oliver Get rid of – ? You mean – ? (*He holds his head in his hands.*) So I'm too late . . .

Reg I told him we had to give ourselves up. I said we were only making it worse for ourselves, I raised a whole lot of quite persuasive arguments. That's why he tied me up, because I wanted out of this crazy business. But all he cared about was the money.

Oliver The money? Oh, the money! (*He jabs a finger demonically at Reg.*) Where's all the money, scumbag?

Reg Well, well, I spent my share, I'm not proud of that, but the truth is I've spent every penny, Officer. I'm unproud of that.

Oliver What on?

Reg Denzil Golden records.

Oliver Who's Denzil Golden?

Reg He's a singer. More than a singer though, he's . . . Look, could you untie me? I think I've damaged my back and my trousers are wet through with all this high stress pressure.

Oliver No way, I wasn't born yesterday. (*Thinks about it for a second.*) Well, alright, but any funny business and I'll have you in the cuffs. Scumbag.

Reg Oh, I won't try anything, officer, I promise.

Oliver starts to untie him.

I'm not normally such a villain, not so long ago I had a job and . . . I guess my love of Denzil's music clouded my judgement . . . (*He's free now.*) Ahhh! Thank you, thanks.

Reg goes and picks up one of his beloved broken records.

Boy, look at this. A red vinyl Chemical Toilet, gone for ever.

Oliver You stole someone's dead mum just to buy these old records?

Reg drops to his knees to pick up the broken pieces.

Reg They're more than records to me, Officer, I know it sounds sort of sentimental, but – oh God, Diabolical Chariots . . .

He holds up two pieces of a record and tries to fit them together.

Would these still play, do you think, if I glued them carefully? Is that worth a try? Do you think, officer?

But Oliver is engrossed in an album sleeve he's picked up – 'The Greatest Hits Of Denzil Golden' – with a big picture of Denzil Golden on it.

Oliver Is this him? This Denzil Golden?

Reg Yes, but that's not much of a record, they just put that out to cash in on his memory when he choked on his own vomit.

Oliver What did you say the names of those albums were?

Reg This one here's Diabolical Chariots. Would this still play if I put it back together with some kind of special record glue?

Oliver And that other one, what's that?

Reg This? Chemical Toilet. I'm never going to find another red vinyl one like that. Green vinyl, maybe, but never another red.

Oliver is pulling out records from Reg's collection.

Oliver . . . Mobile Home-icide . . . Silly Little Fridges . . .

Reg Would you mind being kind of careful there, Officer, some of those are –

Oliver Evidence.

Reg Hm? No, rare I was going to say, rare.

Oliver pulls out his father's notebook and shows it to Reg.

Oliver Recognise this customer here, sir?

Reg Where did you get that, I thought I had every picture of him ever drawn?

Oliver It's an artist's impression. Of a suspect called The Beast UK.

Reg The who? No, I remember him, he went around – He was one of those –

Oliver Caravan-obsessed serial killers, that's right. And look at the titles of these records of yours.

Oliver casually tosses him a record, which he fails to catch.

Diabolical Chariots. Caravans.

Reg Careful! Careful!

Oliver throws another one, which Reg misses again.

Oliver Chemical Toilet. Caravans.

Reg These are fragile!

Oliver throws another.

Oliver Mobile Home-icide. Caravans.

Throws another.

Jazz-Cabbage. Cara – (*Thinks about it a second.*) Well maybe not that one, but the others –

Throws one final record.

Silly Little Fridges – the others are all about caravans, aren't they?

Reg Well now, they're about many things, Officer, they're complicated pieces with subtexts and, and, themes, and symbolism and –

Oliver Chiefly it's caravans though, isn't it. Do you happen to have a sample of this character's writing?

Reg I've got just about everything he ever wrote, or signed. Every scrap of his life is on these shelves – there's a whole letter here, look, from Denzil to his agent –

Reg takes out a letter from a clear plastic protective folder. Oliver snatches it off him and reads it.

Careful! God!

Oliver (*reading*) 'Dear Blood-Sucking Sex Offender. Why haven't I had any money you sinister lesbian weather awful how am I supposed to work in such conditions parasite? Drink my toilet splash-backs, Denzil Golden.'

Reg He had a creative temperament, that doesn't prove anything at all.

Oliver No. But look at this.

Oliver takes out a small folded letter from inside his father's notebook.

This is a letter that an unknown someone wrote to my dad. He investigated the case. The Terrier they called him. Look at the writing. Especially the bit here, where it says 'Drink my toilet splash-backs, The Beast UK.'

Reg (*looking at it*) It's . . . well, it's . . . what strikes you straight away is just how different they are, isn't it, how . . . this one here is obviously in blue ink whereas this one is a completely different colour, black if anything . . . they're chalk and cheese . . .

Oliver stares at him for a second.

Oliver I don't think you're convincing either of us, are you.

Reg Oh God . . .

Oliver Everything points the same way. The Beast UK is Denzil Golden.

Reg . . . One's in blue ink and . . . oh my God . . . D. G. . . . The Beast . . .?

Reg sinks into a chair, devastated.

Oliver Case solved. (*He looks up to the heavens.*) Still the same Dad. Not about to let being dead get in the way of your work. Well, cheers Dad. Here's to the Terrier, who always, always gets his man.

Oliver raises an imaginary glass. Much to his surprise there is a clink sound. He raises his glass again, and the same clink sound is heard. He does this once more, then Leyon enters carrying two bottles which clink together.

Leyton Whatever this fucker's told you is bullshit.

Blackout.

Vaughan's kitchen. Vaughan and Hannah staring out of the window.

Vaughan Look at that, Sweets. Her ash is all over the river, due to that loose lid on the urn.

Hannah I know, Daddy.

Vaughan All mingled up with the beer cans and the driftwood and the shopping trollies. Blending with the frothy scum, Princess.

Hannah But Oliver said . . . he was going to . . . he *promised* (*sighs*) You were right, Daddy. I shouldn't've trusted in him. My weird heart ruled my clever head. He wasn't a saviour after all.

Vaughan If it had just sunk into the river I'd've said it was merely awful. But it coming open like that, I think that smacks of malice.

Hannah I have got toys in my head after all.

Vaughan Smacks of bloody-mindedness even. Just bad luck at random couldn't conspire to have her remains stuck in buttery effluent like that.

Hannah It's all my fault.

Vaughan In what looks like raw industrial waste, chance alone you'd have to say couldn't twist the knife so cleverly. I detect malice in that. Don't you?

Hannah . . . Yes . . .

Vaughan I actually think we could be cursed. Blighted by a hex.

Hannah We're certainly having out fair share of trouble . . .

Vaughan More than our fair share, that's my point Flower. I smell a rat. It takes a brain to come up with evil as pure as this. It takes eyes and hands, it has to be plotted and planned. Which means there must be someone behind it. Or something, doing the plotting and planning.

Hannah Like a bad God?

Vaughan Yes! Or maybe a whole bunch of them, ganging up on us. I smell a big smelly rat.

Hannah Is that good news or bad news, Daddy?

Vaughan Well it's a bit of both, isn't it, it's a custard pie full of broken glass, but it means we're not to blame. None of this happened just because I left your mother in the park. I was fated to do that.

Hannah It's not my fault I mistook that stupid fat clumsy oaf for a hero, and that by doing so Mummy ended up in the effluent?

Vaughan Nope! You had no choice.

Hannah That's definitely good news. We haven't made awful mistakes.

Vaughan We were doomed from the start! Everything we've done was scripted for us, we just acted it out. Look, look at this!

He shakes the dresser violently. The photograph of his wife falls and breaks.

Before I just did that, who could've said which object'd break?

Hannah Not me, Daddy.

Vaughan Nor me! But someone knew. It wasn't random, someone decided it'd be your mother's picture instead of – this plate, say.

He picks up a plate from the dresser and smashes it.

Vaughan It could've been that just as easily.

Hannah We're not in control of anything we're doing!

Vaughan Not a thing!

Hannah Because we're cursed!

Vaughan Doomed!

Hannah Fantastic! It's an acquittal!

Vaughan It's all pre-planned! Even if I suddenly do this –

He begins to leap about and ribbit like a frog, waving his arms above his head.

– I'm not fooling anyone! Not even this is unplanned!

Hannah It's not spontaneous, however out of character it looks to me!

Vaughan It's fated!

Hannah Even though it looks a bit madcap!

Vaughan Predestined! Thank goodness, Sweets, we never had a chance!

Hannah Good news at last!

Vaughan Yes!

Hannah Tinged with sadness, maybe, but you can't expect fairy-tales!

Vaughan It's not that sort of environment!

She joins him in his demented frog impersonation.

Hannah Daddy, in a funny way, it's good news at last!

Lights fade.

SCENE TWENTY

Reg's lounge. Leyton, Reg and Oliver.

Leyton He found the urn, he was the brains behind the thing.

Reg The brains, oh come on now, that's a porky pie you're telling –

Oliver Where's the urn now, that's all I want to know? (*Looks at his hand.*) You pair of scumbags.

Leyton What urn? There is no urn, what urn at all, no urn here?

Reg He probably threw it away, officer –

Leyton Shut up Reg! He told me to throw it away. The mastermind here. Throw it off Corp's Bridge, he said, and throw it good, sonny.

Reg 'Throw it good, sonny', that doesn't even sound like the way I speak.

Leyton I was just following fucking orders. Throw the urn good and far, the evil genius here said. What was I to do?

Reg Boy oh boy Leyton . . . fair's fair now . . .

Oliver crosses to the window and stares out of it mournfully.

Oliver You threw her off the bridge . . .?

Leyton I was following Reg's orders. He'd've fuckin smoked me otherwise.

Leyton mimes it and makes a gunshot sound.

Back of the head job.

He mimes it again.

Oliver . . . Into the river . . .? (*sighs*) Well, yeah, that figures. I'm the kiss of death, me. The minute I got involved it was always going to end in tears. They should've let me drown. They'll regret it now. Now that she's in the river instead of me.

He turns to face them, and begins to take off his helmet. Places it down, undoes his top button. Puffs out his chest and two buttons ping off.

Reg I want to put on record just how sorry I am, Officer, I can see this has upset you.

Leyton I'm the impressionable guy you get in these kind of things, the naive guy who doesn't know what he's getting himself into.

Oliver And to think for a minute I actually kidded myself she might be right. I thought I might be the new Plennie Wingo. I even thought I could be Sir Temulji to her Lady Nariman.

Leyton Huh? Sir who?

Oliver Longest-ever recorded marriage, eighty-six years from 1853 to – Well, it doesn't matter. Not now.

Reg I don't even mind going to prison I feel so bad about this, Officer.

Oliver I guess I just let someone down, that's all. Nothing new in that. A couple of broken hearts to add to the list of Bad Stuff I've caused.

Leyton Jesus, it was only fucking ash.

Silence descends. Oliver looks at him.

Oliver (*to Leyton*) What?

Reg This is what I've been saying, Officer, this brother of mine behaves like a heck of a goblin sometimes.

Oliver (*to Leyton*) What did you just say?

Leyton Nothing, I said nothing –

Oliver It was only ash?

Leyton Fuck no, not me, holy mash I said, you misheard me.

Oliver paces pensively.

Holy mash I said.

Oliver In a way, though, that's true . . . It *was* only ash. I mean, it's what someone puts in to something that makes it important, you take that away and what are you left with, you're left with ash, that's what . . .

Leyton That's what I said, it was only ash, there you fucking go.

Oliver . . . I mean if we left the dead wherever they dropped the kestrels would have a field day, and we're too warm-blooded to let that happen. So we have a funeral to show that the remains are more than just an old carcass because that lump was once a human being, and that matters – if not to nature or God or anything else, then at least to a few other human beings.

Leyton No, you've fucking lost me now.

Oliver It's not what's left, it's what's *gone* that's important. The actual bones, or the ash or whatever, that's just so much calcium and carbon. And all that's been lost here is exactly that, a pot of ash. What's gone is still there in the hearts of her loved ones. It's those human hearts that change a pile of ash into . . . something more than that.

Leyton It was just fucking ash, we're all agreed, there's no such crime as ash-throwing, end of story.

Reg Whether there is or not, Leyton, it's just not nice, we should both be ashamed of ourselves.

Oliver looks at his hand. Begins to gently rub at the words on it.

Oliver You wouldn't happen to have a barbecue, would you?

Leyton Huh . . .? Yeah we have, you go ahead and grill some stuff, there's some beer in the fridge too –

Oliver No, no, I'm not hungry, sir. I just want a bag of ash.

Leyton A fucking what sorry?

Reg Oh come on now, Officer, is that wise . . .?

Oliver Sir, please, I'm following official procedure in a case like this. If you can get me a bag of ash then you're both free to go.

Leyton Right, fuck yeah, it's coming – bag of ash, it's coming right up here, one bag of ash . . .

Leyton exits speedily.

Reg I guess you know what you're doing, Officer, but this seems a little bit strange to me.

Oliver I have a responsibility to the victims of this crime. They put their faith in me. Well, one of them did, the other one barely concealed his contempt but Hannah . . .

Hannah looked up to me. She really believed I was capable of anything. When I saw the admiration in her eyes, I thought it was a miracle. But it wasn't, as it happens. It was just the moment I'd waited for all my life.

Reg I see what you're saying, and I don't mean to criticise. I'm a man in a glass house and I'm not going to make the basic mistake of throwing stones.

Oliver I have to ask you not to mention the urn going over the side of the bridge though. That's a routine request in this type of case.

Reg Anything you say.

Oliver And I'm also going to have to ask you to go to the station and tell them about Denzil Golden.

Reg First thing tomorrow, you have my word.

Oliver Tell them Romulous Hoff sent you.

Reg Right, that's you is it? Romulous Hoff?

Oliver (*smiles*) Yes. In a way, I think it is, sir.

Reg Well that's more than fair, officer, that's a let-off compared to what we deserve.

Leyton returns with the bag of ash.

Oliver Of course, we haven't mentioned all the money you took from Hannah and her Dad.

Leyton Who? Oh, those two. Well we were just accepting a reward for a lost item.

Reg No, no – we'll repay every penny of that, officer, one way or another. Even if I have to sell my Denzil Golden records.

Oliver You'll have to check with my colleagues at the station before you sell any of these.

Leyton The station? You said we were fucking free to go, look I got covered in fucking ash here –

Leyton gives Oliver the bag of ash.

Reg The officer found out something about Denzil, Leyton, something really bad. It turns out Denzil . . . It seems D. G. . . . he . . .

Oliver Denzil Golden is none other than the notorious mass murderer known as The Beast UK.

Leyton What?

Reg It's true! It's true, Leyton, oh God help us it's true.

Leyton What – ? This guy – ? With all these crap songs, he's The Beast?

Oliver 'Fraid so sir.

Leyton Oh Jesus!

Reg It's awful, isn't it, God help us . . .

Leyton Holy, holy shit and – then the records . . . oh shit . . .

Reg You're actually taking this a bit worse than I thought, Leyton, I guess you grew to love his music too, huh?

Leyton leaps up and begins counting the records.

Leyton, what you doing, you're not going to break any more of my records are you?

Leyton *Break* them? Have you got any idea how much these things are *worth*? Why'd you let me smash stuff that was priceless?

Reg Well now I said at the time they were rare, Leyton. I used the word 'irreplaceable' more than once.

Leyton I thought you just meant *musically*. Not in money terms.

Reg I do mean that, they're not worth much financially.

Leyton Are you kidding? There's thousands of people like me with an unhealthy interest in this kind of stuff, it's a goldmine. Love songs sung by a serial killer, have you got any idea what *Motiveless Crimes* would pay for ghoulish stuff like this? Jesus! You got signed photos!

He picks up some Denzil Golden signed photos.

Reg I got one or two, yes, but –

Leyton One or two?

Reg Thirty or so, but listen to me –

Leyton Thirty? Jesus Christ! We'll get a grand each for them!

Reg Oh I'm not sure glorifying the man's undoubted character flaws is really ethical, Leyton. I'm all for bringing the man's music to a wider audience but even as a genuine fan I find his behaviour *vis à vis* mass slaughter just completely reprehensible.

Oliver Well, I suppose if selling these records meant you could pay back Hannah and Vaughan, then . . . morally, I suppose that . . .

Reg I guess that wouldn't be so bad, would it, Officer? If we paid back say double what we took, then . . .?

Oliver I think they'd appreciate that. I think that way everyone comes out of this with something.

He picks up his helmet.

Reg That's more than fair. And tell them how sorry we are, won't you?

Oliver I will do. And, er, I'll be keeping an eye on this case, just so you know. They don't call me The Terrier for nothing.

Reg and Oliver shake hands. Oliver exits. Leyton waves a letter at Reg.

Leyton Letters? You've got letters? How many, Reg? How many?

Lights fade.

SCENE TWENTY-ONE

Vaughan's kitchen. Vaughan tucking into swan sandwiches like a man possessed. Hannah looking out of the window with the telescope. Vaughan belches loudly.

Vaughan That's me done, Flower. Pw, I must have hollow legs or a giant stringy tapeworm in my belly.

Belches again.

Hannah There are a hundred and fourteen people on the bridge, Daddy. And a dog.

Vaughan Is that a media scrum or a media circus, I always get those two confused?

Hannah Whichever it is, there's an awful lot of cameras.

Vaughan gets up and joins her at the window.

Vaughan Well it'll be nice if the publicity does stop people jumping, Princess. I've had enough of that splish, splish, splish sound night and day.

Hannah What will be will be, I suppose.

Vaughan Absolutely. Whatever the hex decrees.

A knock at the door.

Will either of us puppets answer that?

Hannah Only time will tell.

Short silence.

Yes, it turns out I'll go.

Hannah goes and answers the door. It's Oliver, carrying the ash. Hannah turns away with utter indifference.

Hannah (*bored, almost*) It's Oliver.

Vaughan Ah. Look at me shrug, look.

He shrugs.

See it?

Hannah Yes.

Vaughan I'm off to watch the melee a minute. You coming?

Hannah I don't seem to be. Maybe later though.

Vaughan exits outside. Hannah sits down, and Oliver edges nervously into the room.

Oliver It's crazy up there. One of them asked me if I'd seen Oliver Hoff. Apparently he's six foot seven with blond wavy hair.

Hannah I'm slightly surprised that you've got the nerve to show your big lard arse, although I suppose it was inevitable that you would, given the fact that everything that happens is inevitable. Mr Wobbly.

Oliver Riiiiiight . . . Don't worry, I'm used to hostility, this is familiar ground. I just thought I'd pop in to return the remains of your mother and tell you that the two scumbags will repay you double all the money that they took off you, and would like to apologise for everything they've done to you and your Dad.

He puts the ash down on the table and begins to exit.

Hannah I don't think I quite heard that right.

Oliver (*stopping*) That'll be me muttering again, I do that. (*louder*) I just thought I'd pop in to return the remains of –

Hannah suddenly gets to her feet.

Hannah Because we saw the man throw Mummy off the bridge earlier.

Oliver Ohhhh . . . you, er, you saw that did you . . .? Well . . . the thing is . . . one of the evil scumbags had . . . had, yes, one of them had switched the remains of your mother with a bag of ash from the barbecue. And, and that's what you saw being thrown from the bridge.

Hannah Ash? From a barbecue? So . . . so in the bag is . . .?

Oliver This is the human stuff, yes. (*Beat.*) Sorry, I can't believe I just said 'the human stuff', I'm straight out of a circus sometimes.

Hannah Mummy? In a bag? Like a goldfish?

Oliver Yes, I'm sorry about the container, I realise there's a deficit of dignity there, but . . . well it's the ash that's important, isn't it? That's what really matters, is the . . . ash.

Hannah looks at him and back at the bag for a second.

Hannah It's impossible not to hug you. I doubted you and now suddenly 'sorry' is too many words.

She hugs him, for a longer period of time than you'd think, and he smiles.

Oliver Wow. This is great. I can't remember the last time someone hugged me. Part of me doesn't want this moment to ever end. The other part of me is covered in a weird rash that is agonisingly painful.

Hannah releases him.

Hannah Sorry.

Oliver No, it's this, er, jacket, I don't normally wear synthetic materials.

Hannah Oh no. Oh. I've suddenly become a little crest-fallen, I think.

Oliver Have you?

Hannah Yes, a bit, on account of all the ramifications.

Oliver Sorry, I'm as thick as two short planks, ramifi – ?

Hannah If this is Mummy, in a bag like a mad dead gold-fish, then the lid coming off the urn means nothing, and there's no hex, planned by no-one and the self-same no-one hasn't got it in for us or anyone else. We were just unlucky. And it's all our fault, even if it doesn't serve us right. It was Daddy's fault that he left Mummy in the park, and the frog impression becomes a lot more embarrassing.

Oliver I see what you mean.

Hannah You do?

Oliver No.

Hannah We were out of our minds, you see, and we liked it better than when we were in them. Daddy developed a shrug.

Oliver I saw that.

Hannah And had a kind of faith, that everything was not going to be alright. I think a happy ending might shake his whole belief in fate, and we'd be right back where we started. All ad-hoc, and broken. It's a little paradoxical, but good news is the last thing we need right now.

Oliver Right. So, in short, I got it wrong again?

Hannah Not necessarily.

Hannah takes the ash and begins to pour it down the sink.

Oliver What are you doing?

Hannah I'm pouring Mummy down the sink.

Oliver You can't do that! Stop it, stop!

Hannah I'll apologise to her later.

Oliver Wait! Stop!

Hannah She has to go, actually. Please let go of my – Please, you'll –

Oliver tries to wrestle the ash off Hannah and it goes all over both of them. Vaughan re-enters as this happens but neither of them notice him. He picks up the telescope.

Now she's everywhere.

Oliver Oh God.

Hannah Now I've got Mummy in my hair, for example.

Oliver I'm so sorry.

Vaughan Mummy?

Hannah and Oliver both give cries of surprise. Vaughan gently puts down the telescope.

What do you mean, Sweets, 'Mummy'? She's . . . she wasn't . . .?

Hannah I feel a bit sick again.

Vaughan We had her back after all and . . . You . . . you were trying to put your mother down the sink . . .?

Hannah Yes. In the nicest possible way, though.

Oliver There's still quite a lot of her 'round the plug-hole. I really think there's a head and two arms worth in here that could be . . . with a bit of effort . . .

He shows a couple of slimy fingers' worth he's dug out of the wet sink.

Vaughan I'm wondering where the dignity is in all this, Princess?

Hannah Nowhere.

Vaughan The buttery effluent suddenly looks like a rose garden, Angel. Resting place of the gods now I've seen the plughole option.

Hannah This is what happens when good intentions backfire all over the place . . . you see Oliver did rescue Mummy after all.

Vaughan He did?

Hannah I always said he was a hero.

Vaughan You did, yes. I had him down as hopeless.

Oliver Well strictly speaking, you know –

Hannah And I thought, given that we'd faced up to losing Mummy so well earlier and accepted we were hexed by a gang of bad gods, that it would be a backwards step to start the whole grief-stricken thing again –

Vaughan I see. So now, not only is your mother down the sink and in your hair, but it's also entirely our fault. And nothing to do with destiny. Just us, and our decisions.

Hannah Yes.

Vaughan No acquittal.

Hannah No.

Vaughan The frog dance is obviously more embarrassing in that case.

Hannah Yes.

Vaughan Well. I would very much like to die now, before anything else has a chance to happen.

Oliver I felt like that once.

Vaughan Yes, and it's a shame you didn't do something more negative about it.

Hannah Daddy!

Oliver You're right. This is all my fault. You see this isn't your wife, Vaughan, this is just ash from a barbecue. When I got to Diesel Terrace and they told me that they'd thrown the urn from the bridge out there, I panicked. I didn't want to let Hannah down, so I got some ash and pretended I'd managed to return your wife.

Hannah You weren't a hero?

Oliver No. Sorry, Hannah. I'm just a salesman with a weight problem.

Vaughan And something of a liar too.

Oliver Yes. A liar too.

Vaughan Well thank God for that. We *are* hexed.

Hannah Even more hexed than we thought. (*She sighs.*) That was a sigh of relief.

Vaughan I thought so.

Hannah In case maybe you thought I was bored.

From outside, the sound of a bridge collapsing.

Oliver What was that?

Vaughan (*looks out of window with telescope. Turns back*) The bridge's anti-collapse mechanisms just failed. Through sheer weight of interest it looks like.

Hannah That's a shame.

Vaughan Yes. Hell of a walk round from now on. I might go and see if I can grab any stunned fish.

He starts to exit outside.

You two ought to think about a wash. We mightn't have free-will, but there's such a thing as hygiene.

Vaughan exits outside. Silence.

Oliver I'm, er . . . I think I know what you're probably thinking . . .

Hannah I'm wondering whether it's possible to admire you enough.

Oliver Sarcasm, well I deserve that I suppose . . .

Hannah Whether maybe awe isn't more appropriate.

Oliver I'll just go, shall I? Or would you like a chance to tell me what you think of me?

Hannah You've changed everything for good and for the better, with the most cunning and lovely white lie a man ever told. You sacrificed your hero's reputation to protect me and spare Daddy from an ugly revelation.

So now I think even more highly of you, and he still has his life-enhancing trust in doom. Because you *did* rescue Mummy, didn't you?

Oliver Er . . . is it better if I *did* rescue her or didn't?

Hannah If you *did*, silly.

Oliver Wasn't it the other way around a minute ago?

Hannah Yes. The situation changes from moment to moment.

Oliver So just so I'm clear on this now: if none of that were true and I really had failed to bring your mother home and then just told the truth about it; if that were the case, would you want to know?

Hannah If you were a lying also-ran?

Oliver For the sake of argument?

Hannah looks at her hand, and rubs off the writing.

Hannah Most things that come to light are dark. And not everything we're not told doesn't help.

Oliver Got you.

Hannah And, of course, vice-versa.

Oliver Right. Yes. Good.

A brief pause.

Well, I suppose I'd better be getting off.

Hannah Where to?

Oliver Ohhh you know. The wide open road. I've got places to see, people to help. Other problems to solve.

Hannah Have you?

Brief pause.

Oliver No. Can I stay here?

Hannah Yes.

> *Music. The lights fade to a pleasant shade of blue,
> under which a montage of images occurs.*
>
> *Vaughan enters, dragging the motionless Margot,
> who is dressed as her mother, in a long red wig and an
> eye-patch. Hannah goes to help, and Margot gradually
> recovers, unearthing a manual typewriter from a large
> handbag. Hannah gets her a glass of water, while
> Vaughan nurses his back and stiffly sits down.*
>
> *Simultaneously, in Reg's lounge, Reg and Leyton
> dance to the music of Denzil Golden. Leyton kisses
> an album cover as he dances. They dance at first
> separately, then together in a bizarre partnership,
> gradually invading the space of Vaughan's kitchen
> until the two worlds are blurred. Throughout all this,
> Oliver stands centre stage, smiling kindly at the
> audience.*
>
> *The lights fade to black.*
> *The End.*